33 enfants

From Jordan to Pentecost

by Derek Prince

"For John truly baptized with water; but ye shall be baptized with the Holy Ghost."

Acts 1:5

"The doctrine of baptisms"

Hebrews 6:2

ISBN NO. 0-934920-02-8

TABLE OF CONTENTS

DEREK PRINCE

King's Scholar, Eton College
B.A., M.A. Cambridge
Formerly
Fellow of King's College,
Cambridge

ABOUT THE AUTHOR

Derek Prince was born in India, of British parents. He was educated as a scholar of Greek and Latin at two of Britain's most famous educational institutions - Eton College and Cambridge University. From 1940 to 1949, he held a Fellowship (equivalent to a resident professorship) in Ancient and Modern Philosophy at King's College, Cambridge. He also studied Hebrew and Aramaic, both at Cambridge University and at the Hebrew University in Jerusalem. In addition, he speaks a number of other modern languages.

In the early years of World War II, while serving as a hospital attendant with the British Army, Derek Prince experienced a life-changing encounter with Jesus Christ, concerning which, he writes:

> Out of this encounter, I formed two conclusions which I have never since had reason to change: first, that Jesus Christ is alive; second, that the Bible is a true, relevant, up-to-date book. These two conclusions radically and permanently altered the whole course of my life.

At the end of World War II, he remained where the British Army had placed him - in Jerusalem. Through his marriage to his first wife, Lydia, he became father to the eight adopted girls in Lydia's children's home there. Together, the family saw the rebirth of the State of Israel in 1948.

While serving as educator in Kenya, Derek and Lydia adopted their ninth child, an African baby girl. Lydia died in 1975, and Derek Prince married his present wife, Ruth, in 1978.

In the intervening years, Derek Prince has served as pastor, educator, lecturer, and counselor on several continents, and is internationally recognized as one of the leading Bible expositors of our time. He has authored over 20 books, many of which have been translated into other languages. In great demand as a conference speaker, Derek Prince travels frequently to many other parts of the world, and also maintains a base in Israel.

Non-denominational and non-sectarian in his approach, Derek Prince has prophetic insight into the significance of current events in the light of Bible prophecy.

\

*   *   *   *   *

With a few changes, these messages are printed here exactly as they were delivered over the air on the Study Hour radio program.

I
The Doctrine Of Baptisms—A

The Verb "Baptize"—Origin, History, Meaning—Four Different Kinds Of Baptism

Welcome to the Study Hour.

Our textbook—the Bible.

Once again we present to you the Bible's own challenge: "Study for yourself." Take time to find out for yourself what the Bible really teaches. It is not enough to accept secondhand opinions, or traditions. You need to get personally acquainted with the great basic themes of the Bible.

The study which we shall now bring you is No. 17 in our present series, entitled "Foundations".*

We are at present working our way systematically through the six great foundation doctrines of the Christian faith, as stated in Hebrews chapter 6, verses 1 and 2. The six doctrines there listed as the "beginning", or "foundation", of the doctrine of Christ are as follows: No. 1, "repentance from dead works"; No. 2, "faith toward God"; No. 3, "the doctrine of baptisms"; No. 4, "laying on of hands"; No. 5, "resurrection of the dead"; No. 6, "eternal judgment."

In our previous studies we have been examining the first two of these six doctrines—that is, "repentance from dead works" and "faith toward God"—or, more simply, "repentance" and "faith." In our present study we shall move on to the third of these great foundation doctrines—that which is called "the doctrine of baptisms."

The logical way in which to begin this particular study is to discover, if possible, the correct, original meaning of the word "baptism"—or, more accurately, of the verb "to baptize," from which the noun "baptism" is formed.

The first sixteen studies in this series are published as two successive books, under the titles: "FOUNDATION FOR FAITH"; "REPENT AND BELIEVE." See the list on back cover of this book.

Upon examination, this word "baptize" proves to be a most unusual and interesting word. Actually it is not an English word at all. It is a pure Greek word, merely written in letters of the English alphabet. If we write out the original Greek word in English letters, as accurately as it is possible to do, this gives us *"baptizo"*. Then, with the change of the final "o" to an "e," we have the word in the form which has become familiar—"baptize".

At this point someone may reasonably ask: "Why was this particular word never translated? Why was it simply written over from Greek to English letters? Was it because the correct meaning of the original Greek word was not known, and therefore the translators did not know by what English word to translate it?"

No, this is definitely not the explanation. As we shall see in due course, the Greek word *"baptizo"* has a perfectly definite and well-established meaning.

In order to clear up the unusual circumstances connected with the use of this word "baptize," it is necessary to glance for a moment at the historical background of Bible translation. By far the best known and the most influential of all the English translations of the Bible is that known as the "King James Version"—the version which was translated and published through the authority of King James of Britain, in the early years of the seventeenth century. It is through this translation that the word "baptize" has gained a place in the English language; and through this King James Version the word "baptize" has been carried over into the great majority of all subsequent English versions of the Bible, as well as into a great many translations of the Bible that have been made into the languages of many different tribes and peoples in various parts of the world. Yet this word "baptize," both in its origin and in its form, is in fact completely alien to almost all those languages.

We may ask then: How did this unusual and unnatural form first find its way into the King James Version of the Bible? The answer lies in the fact that King James, though holding political power as an absolute monarch, was answerable in matters of religion to the bishops of the established Church of England. Now the relationship between James and his bishops was not always too cordial, and James did not wish the new translation of the Bible, published in his name and with his authority, to make his relationship with his bishops any worse. For this reason, he allowed it to be understood that, so far as possible, nothing was to be introduced into the translation which would cause unnecessary offence to the bishops or which would be too obviously contrary to the practices of the established church. Hence, the Greek word *"baptizo"*, which could easily have become, in translation, a source of controversy, was never translated at all, but was simply written over direct into the English language.

In this connection, it is interesting to remark that the very word "bishop" is another example of precisely the same influences at work. In actual fact, the word "bishop" is no more an English word than the word "baptize." "Bishop" is just another Greek word that has been taken over, without translation, into the English language; but in this case it has come by a slightly less direct route, by way of Latin. If the Greek original of the word "bishop" had been translated, everywhere it occurs in the New Testament, by its natural and correct translation—which is "overseer"—the resulting version could have been interpreted as a challenge to the hierarchical order of government that existed in the established Church of England. Therefore, in various places, the translators avoided the issue, and simply left the Greek word to stand in its anglicised form—"bishop."

However, let us now return to the word with which we are directly concerned in this study—the Greek word *"baptizo"*, and its English equivalent "baptize." This Greek verb *"baptizo"* is of a special, characteristic form of which there are a good many other examples in the Greek language. The characteristic feature of this verbal form is the insertion of the two letters "i z" into a more simple, basic root. Thus, the simple, basic root is—*"bapto"*. The insertion into this root of the two extra letters—"i z"—produces the compound form—*"baptizo"*. We find then that the simple, basic root is *"bapto"*. The compound form, produced from that root, is *"baptizo"*.

Now the insertion of the additional syllable, "iz," into any Greek verb normally gives the compound verb thus formed a particular kind of meaning. The insertion of this extra syllable produces a verb that has a special, **causative** meaning. That is to say, the compound verb thus formed always has the sense of **causing** something to be, or to happen. The precise nature of that which is thus caused to be, or to happen, is decided by the meaning of the simple root verb, out of which the compound, causative form has been built up.

With this in mind, we can now form a clear and accurate picture of the Greek verb *"baptizo."* This is a compound, causative form, built up out of the simple, root form, *"bapto"*. Obviously, therefore, to get a proper understanding of the compound, causative form *"baptizo"*, it is necessary first of all to find out the meaning of the simple root form *"bapto"*. Fortunately, there is no difficulty whatever in doing this. This simple root form *"bapto"* occurs three times in the Greek text of the New Testament which forms the basis of the English King James Version. In every one of these three instances the original Greek verb *"bapto"* is translated by the same English verb—and that is the English verb "to dip".

The three New Testament passages in which this word *"bapto"* occurs are as follows:

First, Luke's Gospel, chapter 16, verse 24. Here the rich man, in the torments of hell fire, cries out to Abraham: "Father Abraham, have mercy on me, and send Lazarus, that he may **dip** the tip of his finger in water, and cool my tongue . . ."

Second, John's Gospel, chapter 13, verse 26. Here, at the last supper, Jesus identifies the traitor, who is to betray Him, by giving His disciples a definite, distinguishing mark: "Jesus answered, He it is, to whom I shall give a sop, when I have **dipped** it."

Third, Revelation chapter 19, verse 13. Here John the Revelator describes the Lord Jesus Christ as he sees Him coming forth in glory, leading the avenging armies of heaven: "And he was clothed with a vesture **dipped** in blood."

In all these three passages, both the English word used by the translators, and also the actual context of each passage, plainly show the meaning of the Greek verb *"bapto"*. In each case, it means **"to dip something into a fluid, and then take it out again."**

In that standard work of Biblical reference—Dr. Strong's "Exhaustive Concordance of the Bible"—Dr. Strong gives the following as the primary meaning of the verb *"bapto"*; "to cover wholly with fluid"—hence, "to dip."

We also find in the New Testament a compound version of the verb *"bapto,"* formed by prefixing the Greek preposition *"en"*, or *"em"*—meaning "in". This gives the compound form *"embapto"*. This compound form, *"embapto"*, also occurs three times in the Greek text of the New Testament. The three passages are as follows: Matthew chapter 26, verse 23; Mark chapter 14, verse 20; and John chapter 13, verse 26 (the second half of the verse). Any student who cares to check for himself will quickly discover that in all these three passages this compound form *"embapto"* is translated, just like the simple form *"bapto"*, by the English verb "to dip".

We thus arrive at the following conclusion. The Greek verb *"bapto"*—either in its simple form, or with the prefix of the preposition *"em"* meaning "in"—occurs six times in the Greek text of the New Testament, and in every instance in the King James Version it is translated "to dip". In every instance, also, the context plainly indicates that the action described by this verb is that of **dipping something into a fluid, and then taking it out again.**

Having thus arrived with absolute definiteness at the correct meaning of the simple verb *"bapto"*, there is no difficulty whatever in going on from there to discover, with equal definiteness, the correct meaning of the causative compound form *"baptizo"*. If *"bapto"* means "to dip something into a fluid, and then take it out again," then *"baptizo"* can have only one possible, literal meaning. Logically, it must mean "to cause something to be dipped into a fluid, and then taken out again." More briefly, *"baptizo"*—from which we get the English word "baptize"

—means "to cause something to be dipped."

This conclusion can be confirmed by tracing the word *"baptizo"* back into the earlier history of the Greek language. In the third century before the Christian era the extensive conquests of Alexander the Great had had the effect of spreading the use of the Greek language far beyond the actual geographical confines of Greece herself, or even of the Greek cities and communities of Asia Minor. In this way, by the time of the New Testament, the Greek language had become the generally accepted medium of communication for most of the peoples in the lands bordering on the Mediterranean Sea. It is this form of the Greek language which is found in the New Testament and which traces its origin, linguistically, back to the purer form of classical Greek originally used by the Greek cities and states in the preceding centuries. Thus most of the words used in New Testament Greek trace their origin and their meaning back to the earlier forms of classical Greek.

This is true of the word with which we are at present concerned—the verb *"baptizo"*. This word can be traced back into the earlier, classical form of the Greek language as far as the fifth century B. C. From then on it has a continuous history in the Greek language right down into the first and second centuries A. D. (that is, throughout the whole period of the New Testament writings). Throughout this period of six or seven centuries, the word retains one unchanging basic meaning: "to dip," "to plunge," "to submerge." In this sense, it may be used either literally or metaphorically.

The following are some examples of its use throughout this period:

In the fifth or fourth century B. C. *"baptizo"* is used by Plato of a young man being **"overwhelmed"** by clever philosophical arguments.

In the writings of Hippocrates (attributed to the fourth century B. C.) *"baptizo"* is used of people being **"submerged"** in water, and of sponges being **"dipped"** in water.

In the Septuagint (the Greek version of the Old Testament attributed to the second or first century B. C.) *"baptizo"* is used to translate the passage, in Second

Kings chapter 5, verse 14, where Naaman went down and "dipped himself" seven times in Jordan. (In this passage *"baptizo"* is used in verse 14, but a different Greek word is used in verse 10, where the King James Version uses "wash." In other words, *"baptizo"* means specifically to "dip oneself," not merely to "wash," without dipping).

In the first century B. C. or A. D. *"baptizo"* is used by Strabo to describe people who cannot swim being **"submerged"** beneath the surface of water (in specific contrast to logs of wood which float on the surface).

In the first century A. D. *"baptizo"* is used by Josephus, metaphorically, to describe a man **"plunging"** a sword into his own neck, and of the city of Jerusalem being **"overwhelmed"** or **"plunged"** to irremediable destruction by internal strife. It is obvious that such metaphorical uses as these would not be possible, unless the literal meaning of the word was already clearly established.

In the first or second century A. D. *"baptizo"* is used twice by Plutarch to describe either the body of a person, or the figure of an idol, being **"immersed"** in the sea.

From this brief linguistic study it will be seen that the Greek word *"baptizo"* has always had one clear, definite meaning, which has never changed. From Classical Greek right down into New Testament Greek it has always retained one and the same basic meaning: "to cause something to be dipped"—"to immerse something beneath the surface of water, or of some other fluid." In most cases this act of immersion is temporary, not permanent.

If further confirmation of this be desired, it may be obtained by an altogether different linguistic route. Those who are of Scandinavian background, or who are in some other way familiar with the three cognate Scandinavian languages—that is, Swedish, Norwegian and Danish—will readily acknowledge that in the New Testament translations in all these three languages, the word rendered in the English version by "baptism" is rendered in these Scandinavian versions by the word *"daab"*. It takes only a moment to see that, by origin, by meaning, and by sound, this Scandinavian word *"daab"* is directly connected with the English word "dip".

I venture to say that any honest person, with adequate linguistic qualifications, who will thoroughly investigate this whole question, can come to only one conclusion: the correct meaning of the word *"baptizo"* --"baptise"-- both in the New Testament and elsewhere, is "to cause something to be dipped".

This brief analysis of the meaning of the word "baptism" brings out two distinctive features which are found everywhere that this word is used in the New Testament. Every baptism, considered as an experience, is both "total" and "transitional." It is "total" in the sense that it involves the whole person and the whole personality of the one being baptized; it is "transitional" in the sense that, for the person being baptized, it marks a transition—a passing out of one stage or realm of experience, into a new stage or realm of experience, never previously entered into.

The act of baptism may thus be compared to the opening and closing of a door. The person being baptized passes through a door, opened up to him by the act of baptism, out of something old and familiar, into something new and unfamiliar; and thereafter the door is closed behind him, and there is no way of returning back through that closed door into the old ways and the old experiences.

* * *

Bearing in mind this picture which we have formed of the nature of baptism, let us turn back once again to the passage where baptism is specified as one of the foundation doctrines of the Christian faith—that is, Hebrews chapter 6, verse 2. We observe that the word "baptism" is here used in the plural, not in the singular. It is "the doctrine of **baptisms**" (plural)—not "the doctrine of baptism" (singular). This indicates plainly that the complete doctrine of the Christian faith includes more than one type of baptism. Following this conclusion out through the pages of the New Testament, we discover that there are actually **four** distinct types of baptism referred to at different points. If we set out these four types of baptism in chronological order, conforming to the order in which they are revealed in the New Testament, we arrive at the following outline:

(First, the baptism preached and practised by John the Baptist—a baptism in water—directly connected with the message and experience of "repentance". This type of baptism is described in Mark's Gospel, chapter 1, verse 4: "John did baptize in the wilderness, and preach the baptism of repentance for the remission of sins."

Second, there is a type of baptism which is not precisely described by any one word in the New Testament, but which we may call the baptism of "suffering". This baptism is referred to by Jesus in Luke's Gospel, chapter 12, verse 50: "I have a baptism to be baptized with; and how am I straitened till it be accomplished." It is also referred to in Mark's Gospel, chapter 10, verse 38. This passage records a request made by the sons of Zebedee to have the privilege of sitting with Christ on His right hand and on His left hand in His glory. To this request Jesus replied with the following question: "Ye know not what ye ask: can ye drink of the cup that I drink of? and be baptized with the baptism that I am baptized with?" It is plain that Jesus here refers to the spiritual and physical surrender that lay ahead of Him as He trod the path to the cross—the surrender of His whole being—spirit, soul and body—to the appointed will of the Father that He might take upon Himself the guilt of the world's sin and then pay by His vicarious sufferings the price required to expiate that sin. By these words Jesus indicated to His disciples that the fulfilment of His plan for their lives would in due course demand of them also a like total surrender of their whole being into the hands of God—even, if need be, for the suffering of death.

The third type of baptism revealed in the New Testament is Christian baptism in water. This is referred to by Christ in Matthew's Gospel, chapter 28, verse 19, where He says to His disciples: "Go ye therefore, and teach all nations, baptizing them in the name of the Father, and of the Son, and of the Holy Ghost." The primary feature which thus distinguishes Christian baptism from the baptism of John the Baptist is that Christian baptism is to be carried out in the full name and authority of the Triune God—Father, Son, and Holy Spirit. This was not so with John's baptism.

The fourth type of baptism revealed in the New Testament is the baptism in the Holy Spirit. In Acts chapter 1, verse 5, Jesus speaks about this baptism, and carefully distinguishes it from baptism in water. He says to His disciples: "For John truly baptized with water; but ye shall be baptized with the Holy Ghost not many days hence." Although in the King James Version the preposition used is "with"—baptized "with" the Holy Ghost—in the actual Greek text the preposition used is "in"—baptized "in" the Holy Ghost. Throughout the entire Greek text of the New Testament there are only two prepositions used with the verb "to baptize." These are "in" and "into." This is in full accord with our conclusion as to the literal meaning of the word "baptize"—"to cause to be dipped, or immersed." In Acts chapter 1, verse 8, Jesus reveals the basic purpose of the baptism in the Holy Ghost. He says: "But ye shall receive power, after that the Holy Ghost is come upon you: and ye shall be witnesses unto me . . ." Primarily, therefore, the baptism in the Holy Ghost is a supernatural enduement with power from on high to be a witness for Christ.

In conclusion, we may summarize once again the four types of baptism: First, the baptism of John, in water, for repentance; second, the baptism of suffering; third, Christian baptism in water, in the name of the Father and of the Son and of the Holy Spirit; fourth, the baptism in the Holy Spirit, a supernatural enduement with power from on high.

In our ensuing studies we shall examine what the New Testament teaches about these types of baptism.

II
The Doctrine Of Baptisms—B

John's Baptism: Repentance And Confession—Christian Baptism: Fulfilling All Righteousness

Welcome to the Study Hour.

Our textbook—the Bible.

It is our aim to present to you the great basic truths of the Bible in such a way that you may be able to form your own conclusions as to what the Bible really teaches. In doing this, we urge you to accept the Bible's own challenge—to "study for yourself."

The study which we shall now bring you is No. 18 in our present series, entitled "Foundations".

We are at present working our way systemtically through the six great foundation doctrines of the Christian faith, as stated in Hebrews chapter 6, verses 1 and 2. The six doctrines there listed as the "beginning", or "foundation", of the doctrine of Christ are as follows: No. 1, "repentance from dead works"; No. 2, "faith toward God"; No. 3, "the doctrine of baptisms"; No. 4, "laying on of hands"; No. 5, "resurrection of the dead"; No. 6, "eternal judgment".

In our previous study we commenced to examine the third of these great foundation doctrines—that which is called "the doctrine of baptisms".

We turned our attention first of all to the actual meaning of the word "baptize", and in this connection we made the following discoveries: The word "baptize" is not actually an English word at all, but simply a Greek verb which was taken over into the English of the King James Version of the Bible, without being translated. This Greek verb *"baptizo"* is a compound, causative form of a simple Greek verb *"bapto"*, which occurs six times in the New Testament. In every one of these six occurrences, in the King James Version, this simple verb *"bapto"* is translated by the English verb "to dip". In Dr. Strong's "Exhaustive Concordance of the Bible", Dr. Strong gives as the primary meaning of the simple verb, *"bapto"*, "to cover wholly with fluid"—hence, "to dip". Thus, the causative form *"baptizo"*, derived from this simple form *"bapto"*, naturally has as its basic, literal meaning, "to cause something to be dipped, or to be immersed." Further research into the history of the word *"baptizo"* indicates that throughout the known history of the Greek language, from the earlier classical Greek down to New Testament times, the word has always retained this same basic meaning— "to cause something to be dipped, or immersed."

In the second part of our previous study we pointed out that, in Hebrews chapter 6, verse 2, the word "baptism" is used in the plural—the "doctrine of **baptisms**" (plural); and we discovered that the New Testament does in fact speak in various places of four different types of baptism. These are as follows: First, the baptism of John, in water, for repentance; second, the baptism of suffering; third, Christian baptism in water, in the name of the Father and of the Son and of the Holy Spirit; fourth, the baptism in the Holy Spirit, a supernatural enduement with power from on high.

We also observed that there are two features of baptism, as described in the New Testament, which are common to each of the four different types of baptism there described. In every case, we found that baptism is, by its nature, first, total; and second, transitional. It is total, in the sense that it involves the whole person and the whole personality of the one being baptized; it is transitional, in the sense that in each case the person being baptized passes out of one stage, or realm of experience, into a new stage, or realm of experience, from which there is afterwards no way of return back to the previous stage.

Of the four types of baptism which we have listed, there is one—the baptism of suffering—which belongs to a more advanced level of spiritual experience than the rest, and therefore does not come within the scope of our present series of studies, which—as the title "Foundations" indicates—are deliberately limited to the basic doctrines and experiences of the Christian faith. For this reason, we shall say nothing more about this baptism of suffering in our present study, but we shall confine our attention to the other three types of baptism; and we shall deal with these in the order in which they are unfolded in the record of the New Testament—that is, first, the baptism of John the Baptist; second, Christian baptism in water; third, the baptism in the Holy Spirit.

* * *

There are probably many Christians who are not fully clear as to the difference between the baptism of John the Baptist on the one hand, and Christian baptism on the other. Therefore it is helpful to begin the study of these two forms of baptism by turning to Acts chapter 19, verses 1 through 5; where these two types of baptism are set forth together, side by side, and the important difference between them is clearly brought out:

"And it came to pass, that, while Apollos was at Corinth, Paul having passed through the upper coasts came to Ephesus: and finding certain disciples,

"He said unto them, Have ye received the Holy Ghost since ye believed? And they said unto him, We have not so much as heard whether there be any Holy Ghost.

"And he said unto them, Unto what then were ye baptized? And they said, Unto John's baptism.

"Then said Paul, John verily baptized with the baptism of repentance, saying unto the people, that they should believe on him which should come after him, that is, on Christ Jesus.

"When they heard this, they were baptized in the name of the Lord Jesus."

Here, in Ephesus, it would seem that Paul encountered a group of people who made themselves known to him as "disciples". At first, Paul took them to be disciples of Christ—that is, Christians—but on closer examination he discovered that they were only disciples of John the Baptist. They had heard and accepted John's message of repentance, and the form of baptism that went with it, but they had hitherto heard nothing of the gospel message centring in the life, death and resurrection of Jesus Christ, or of the Christian form of baptism directly connected with the acceptance of the gospel message. After Paul had explained the message of the gospel to them, these people accepted it, and were once again baptized—this time, the scripture states, "in the name of the Lord Jesus."

This incident shows clearly that the baptism of John and Christian baptism are absolutely distinct in their nature and their significance; and that, once John's ministry had closed and the gospel dispensation had been inaugurated, John's baptism was no longer accepted as being equivalent to, or a substitute for, Christian baptism—but, on the contrary, those who had only received John's baptism were required to be baptized again with full Christian baptism.

If we now turn back to Mark's Gospel, chapter 1, verses 3, 4, and 5, we find a summary of John's message and ministry, with its accompanying form of baptism:

"The voice of one crying in the wilderness, Prepare ye the way of the Lord, make his paths straight.

"John did baptize in the wilderness, and preach the baptism of repentance for the remission of sins.

"And there went out unto him all the land of Judaea, and they of Jerusalem, and were all baptized of him in the river of Jordan, confessing their sins."

In the providence of God, John's message and ministry served two special purposes: first, to prepare the hearts of the people of Israel for the advent and revelation of their long-awaited Messiah, Jesus Christ; second, to provide a kind of dispensational link between the dispensation of the law and the prophets, which was closed by John's own ministry, and the dispensation of the gospel, which was initiated about three years later as a result of the death and resurrection of Jesus Christ. In fulfilling both these purposes of God, John's ministry was of necessity brief and temporary. It did not constitute in itself a dispensation, but merely a period of transition.

In his message and ministry, John made two main demands upon the people: first, repentance; second, public confession of sins. Those who were willing to meet these two conditions were thereafter baptized by John in the river Jordan, as a public testimony that they had repented of their past sins and that they were committing themselves henceforward to lead better lives.

In Mark chapter 1, verse 4, it states: "John did baptize in the wilderness, and preach the baptism of repentance for the remission of sins." The more correct ,and literal translation—given in the margin of the King James Version—states: "John did preach the baptism of repentance unto the remission of sins." This agrees with the words of John himself, in Matthew chapter 3, verse 11: "I indeed baptize you with—or, more literally, in—water unto repentance." We see then that John's baptism was "unto" repentance and "unto" remission of sins. It is most important to establish the meaning of the preposition "unto" when used in this way after the verb "to baptize".

Obviously it does not mean that who were baptized by John only entered into the experience of repentance and forgiveness after they had been baptized. On the contrary, when many of the Pharisees and Sadducees came to John to be baptized, John refused to accept them and demanded that they produce evidence of a real change in their lives before he would baptize them. This is recorded in Matthew chapter 3, verses 7 & 8:

"But when he saw many of the Pharisees and Sadducees come to his baptism, he said unto them, O generation of vipers, who hath warned you to flee from the wrath to come?

"Bring forth therefore fruits meet for repentance."

The alternative version given in the margin for "fruits meet for repentance" is "fruits answerable to amendment of life." In other words, John demanded of them: "Prove first by your actions that there has been a real change in your lives, before you ask me to baptize you."

This proves that John demanded, as we should naturally expect, that those who came to him for baptism should produce evidence in their lives of repentance and remission of sins, before he would baptize them. Plainly, therefore, the phrase "baptism unto repentance and unto remission of sins" should not be taken as indicating that these two inward experiences of repentance and forgiveness only followed after the outward act of being baptized. Rather, it indicates—as the context makes plain—that the outward act of being baptized served as a visible seal and assurance that those being baptized had already passed through the experiences of repentance and forgiveness. Thus, the act of baptism served as an outward seal, giving assurance of an inward transformation which had already taken place.

The clear understanding of this point is of great importance, because this phrase, "to baptize into, or unto," recurs in two subsequent passages of the New Testament— once in connection with Christian baptism in water, and once in connection with the baptism in the Holy Spirit— and in each case we must follow the same principle of interpretation as that already established in regard to John's baptism. However, we shall leave until later the detailed examination of these two subsequent passages.

To return to John's baptism. We may sum up its effects as follows. Those who sincerely met John's conditions enjoyed a real experience of repentance and forgiveness, which was expressed in lives changed for the better. However, these experiences were similar in character to the ministry of John which produced them—they were essentially transitional. Those whom John baptized did not achieve the condition of abiding inward peace and victory over sin, made possible only through the full gospel message of Jesus Christ; but their hearts were prepared to receive and respond to the gospel message when it should be proclaimed.

*   *   *

Let us now turn from the transitional to the permanent —from the baptism of John to full Christian baptism, ordained by Christ Himself as an integral part of the complete gospel message. The passage of scripture which serves best to introduce Christian baptism is that which describes the baptism of Jesus Christ Himself. This is found in Matthew's Gospel, chapter 3, verses 13 through 17:

"Then cometh Jesus from Galilee to Jordan unto John, to be baptized of him.

"But John forbad him, saying, I have need to be baptized of thee, and comest thou to me?

"And Jesus answering said unto him, Suffer it to be so now; for thus it becometh us to fulfil all righteousness. Then he suffered him.

"And Jesus, when he was baptized, went up straightway out of the water: and, lo, the heavens were opened unto him, and he saw the Spirit of God descending like a dove, and lighting upon him:

"And lo a voice from heaven, saying, This is my beloved Son, in whom I am well pleased."

The first point which must be cleared up in connection with this account is that, although Jesus was baptized by John the Baptist, the form of baptism through which He passed was not at all on the same level as that of all the other people whom John baptized. As we have already pointed out, John's baptism made two main demands upon the people: repentance, and confession of sins. However, Jesus Christ had never committed any sins which He needed to confess, or to repent of. Hence, He did not need to be baptized by John in at all the same way as all the other people who came to John for baptism.

John himself clearly recognized this fact, for in the passage which we have just read—in Matthew chapter 3, verse 14—he says: "I have need to be baptized of thee, and comest thou to me?" However, Jesus answers in the next verse: "Suffer it to be so now: for thus it becometh us to fulfil all righteousness."

In this answer of Jesus we find both the reason why Jesus Himself was baptized, and also the true signficance of full Christian baptism, as distinct from the temporary form of baptism administered by John. Jesus was not baptized by John as the outward evidence that He had repented of His sins—because He had no sins to repent of. On the contrary, as Jesus Himself explained, he was baptized in order that he might "fulfil—or complete—all righteousness." In this—as in many other aspects of His life and ministry—Jesus was deliberately and consciously establishing a pattern of behaviour in which He intended that all His believing disciples should thereafter follow Him. By being baptized by John, He was deliberately setting an example and pattern of the baptism in which He desired Christian believers to follow Him.

This is in full accord with the words of the apostle Peter in his First Epistle, chapter 2, verses 21 and 22:

"For even hereunto were ye called: because Christ also suffered for us, leaving us an example, that ye should follow his steps:

"Who did no sin, neither was guile found in his mouth: . . ."

This confirms that which we have already said: Jesus was not baptized by John because He had repented of His sins. On the contrary, as Peter states, Jesus "did no sin, neither was guile found in his mouth." But in being thus baptized, He left an example for all Christians, that they should follow His steps.

With this in mind, let us turn back to the reason which Jesus Himself gave for being baptized, as stated in Matthew chapter 3, verse 15, and let us examine His words there given in greater detail: "Thus it becometh us to fulfil all righteousness."

For the sake of the clearest possible understanding, let us divide up this reason into three sections: First, the word "thus"; second, the phrase, "it becometh us"; third, the concluding section, "to fulfil all righteousness."

First, the word "thus"—or, more plainly, "in this manner". By His example, Jesus established the pattern for the manner, or method, of baptism. Jesus was not baptized as an infant. In Luke chapter 2, verse 22, we read that, while Jesus was still an infant, His parents "brought him to Jerusalem, to present him to the Lord." There is no thought or suggestion here of baptism. Jesus was not baptized until He had come to years of understanding, so that He knew at that time both what He was doing and the reason why He was doing it.

Then again, with further reference to the manner of baptism, we read in the next verse of Matthew chapter 3—that is, Matthew chapter 3, verse 16: "And Jesus, when he was baptized, **went up straightway out of the water**". By simple logic we deduce from this that Jesus, in order to be baptized, first went down into, and then came up out of, the water. Taken in conjunction with the plain, literal meaning of the verb "to baptize" (which we have already discussed), this leaves no reasonable room to doubt that Jesus, in being baptized, suffered Himself to be wholly immersed by John beneath the waters of Jordan.

Let us move on now to the second section of the reason given by Jesus for being baptized: "it becometh us." The phrase, "it becometh", suggests that, for those who would follow Christ, being baptized is something becoming, something fitting, something ordained of God. It is not exactly a legal commandment, such as those imposed upon Israel by the law of Moses, but it is, for Christians, a most natural and becoming expression of sincere and wholehearted discipleship. By using the plural form "us"— "it becometh us"—it would seem that Jesus by anticipation identified Himself with all those of His believing people who would subsequently follow Him through this appointed act of faith and obedience.

Finally, we come to the concluding section: "to fulfil—or to complete—all righteousness." As we have already pointed out, Jesus did not go through the ordinance of baptism as evidence that He had confessed and repented of His sins. On the contrary, He had never committed any sins; He was always perfectly righteous. This righteousness was, in the first instance, an inward condition of heart which Jesus had always possessed. However, in allowing Himself to be baptized, Jesus fulfilled—or completed—this inward righteousness by an outward act of obedience to the will of His heavenly Father; and it was through this outward act of obedience and dedication to God that He actually entered into the active life of ministry by which He fulfilled the plan of God the Father.

So it is with all true, believing Christians who are baptized. Christian believers are not baptized merely because they are sinners who have confessed and repented of their sins. This would be to place Christian baptism right back on the same level as John's baptism. It is true that Christians have confessed and repented of their sins. Without this, they could not be Christians at all. But they have passed beyond this into something much fuller and greater than was ever possible for those who knew only the message and the baptism of John. In Romans chapter 5, verse 1, we read: "Therefore being justified by faith, we have peace with God through our Lord Jesus Christ." True Christians have not merely confessed and repented of their sins. They have done this, and more. By faith in the atoning death and resurrection of Jesus Christ on their behalf, they have been justified—they have been made righteous—the righteousness of Christ Himself has been imputed to them by God on the basis of their faith. And this is the reason why they are then baptized—not simply as evidence that they have confessed and repented of their sins—but in order "to fulfil—to complete—all righteousness"—that is, to make complete, by an outward act of obedience, the inward righteousness which they have already received in their hearts by faith. This explanation shows us how totally different in its true nature and significance is Christian baptism from the baptism which John preached; and we can now understand why the apostle Paul would not accept John's baptism for those who desired to be true Christians, but first instructed them in the full truth of the gospel centring in Christ's death and resurrection, and then insisted on their being baptized once again wih full Christian baptism.

We may now sum up our analysis of the reason which Jesus Himself gave for being baptized. By the word "thus" Jesus established the manner, or method, of baptism: going down into, and coming up out of, the water. By the phrase, "it becometh us", he established a precedent, which it becomes all sincere Christian believers to follow. And by the concluding phrase, "to fulfil all righteousness", He gave the reason: to complete by an outward act of obedience the inward righteousness which the believer already enjoys, by faith, in his heart.

In conclusion we may therefore sum up the nature of

Christian baptism as follows: Christian baptism is an outward act of obedience by which the Christian believer fulfils, or completes, the inward righteousness which he already enjoys in his heart through faith in Christ's atoning death and resurrection.

III
Christian Baptism—A

Conditions For Baptism: Being Taught; Repenting; Believing;
A Good Conscience–Instruction Before Baptism

Welcome to the Study Hour.

Our textbook—the Bible.

Our aim—not to tell you what to believe, but to present to you the doctrines of the Bible in such a way that you may be able to form your own conclusions as to what it really teaches.

The study which we shall now bring you is No. 19 in our present series, entitled "Foundations".

We are at present working our way systematically through the six great foundation doctrines of the Christian faith, as stated in Hebrews chapter 6, verses 1 and 2. The six doctrines there listed as the "beginning", or "foundation", of the doctrine of Christ are as follows: No. 1, "repentance from dead works"; No. 2, "faith toward God"; No. 3, "the doctrine of baptisms"; No. 4, "laying on of hands"; No. 5, "resurrection of the dead"; No. 6, "eternal judgment".

In our last two studies we have been examining the third of these great foundation doctrines—that which is called "the doctrine of baptisms."

In the course of these two studies we have hitherto arrived at the following main conclusions:

First, the Greek verb rendered in the King James Version by the word "to baptize" has one definite, clearly established meaning:—"to cause something to be dipped, or immersed."

Second, the phrase, "the doctrine of **baptisms**" (plural), indicates that more than one kind of baptism is referred to in the New Testament. Upon examination, we discovered four distinct kinds of baptism depicted in the New Testament: the baptism of John the Baptist; the baptism of suffering; Christian baptism in water; the baptism in the Holy Spirit.

Setting aside the baptism of suffering, as being outside the scope of our present studies, we compared and contrasted the baptism of John the Baptist with full Christian baptism.

We saw that John's baptism was a purely temporary provision of God, designed to prepare the people of Israel for the advent of their Messiah, and to mark the period of transition from the dispensation of the law and the prophets to the dispensation of the gospel of Christ. The two conditions imposed upon all those who desired John's baptism were that they should confess, and repent of, their sins. Thereafter, the act of being baptized served as a visible seal and assurance that these two conditions had been duly met.

We saw that Christian baptism differs from John's baptism in two main respects: first, Christian baptism is administered in the full name and authority of the Triune God—Father, Son, and Holy Spirit; second, those receiving Christian baptism have entered into a far greater and fuller spiritual experience than was ever possible for those who knew only the message and the baptism of John. The true Christian believer has not merely confessed and repented of his sins; by faith in Christ's atoning death and resurrection he has been justified, he has received Christ's own righteousness imputed to him by faith. Thereafter, Christian baptism is an outward seal, an outward act of obedience, by which such a believer fulfils, or completes, the inward righteousness which he already enjoys in his heart through his faith in Christ.

We see, then, that the true nature and purpose of Christian baptism are summed up in the words of Jesus at His own baptism, as recorded in Matthew, chapter 3, verse 15: "Thus it becometh us to fulfil—to complete—all righteousness."

* * *

We shall now go on to examine in detail the exact conditions which must be fulfilled by those who desire to receive Christian baptism. We, shall examine, in their logical order, the various passages in the New Testament where these conditions are stated.

The first condition is stated by Christ Himself, in Matthew chapter 28, verses 19 and 20:

"Go ye therefore, and teach all nations, baptizing them in the name of the Father, and of the Son, and of the Holy Ghost:

"Teaching them to observe all things whatsoever I have commanded you: . . ."

We notice that Christ's command to "teach" new converts is here given twice—once before baptizing them, and then again after baptizing them. This is logical and reasonable. Before being baptized, new converts need to receive sufficient teaching to enable them to understand for themselves the nature and the purpose of the ordinance to which they are required to submit themselves. After being baptized, they need to continue to receive further, more thorough and more extensive teaching, in order that they may become strong, intelligent, responsible Christians. Thus, we see that, according to Christ's commandment, teaching must both precede and follow baptism.

The second condition for Christian baptism is stated in Acts chapter 2, verses 37 and 38, which record the reaction of the Jewish multitude to Peter's sermon on the day of Pentecost, and the instructions which Peter thereafter gave them:

"Now when they heard this, they were pricked in their heart, and said unto Peter and to the rest of the apostles, Men and brethren, what shall we do?

"Then Peter said unto them, Repent, and be baptized every one of you in the name of Jesus Christ for the remission of sins, and ye shall receive the gift of the Holy Ghost."

Here in answer to the question, "What shall we do?", the apostle Peter gives two clear and definite commands: first, repent; then, be baptized. Repentance must come first, before baptism. Thereafter, baptism is the outward seal, or assurance, of the inward change that has already been produced by repentance.

The third condition for Christian baptism is stated by Christ Himself, in Mark chapter 16, verses 15 and 16:

"And he said unto them, Go ye into all the world, and preach the gospel to every creature.

"He that believeth and is baptized shall be saved; but he that believeth not shall be damned."

Here Christ states that everywhere the gospel is preached, those that desire to be saved are required to do two things: first, to believe; then, to be baptized.

This condition for baptism is very clearly illustrated in the encounter between Philip and the Ethiopian eunuch, recorded in Acts chapter 8, verses 26 through 39. Here we read how Philip encountered the eunuch on the road from Jerusalem to Gaza; heard him read from the prophet Isaiah; went up and joined him in his chariot; and then preached to him the gospel message of Christ's suffering, death and resurrection, prophetically foreshown by the prophet Isaiah. After some time, as they continued together on their journey, their way led past some water; and upon the eunuch's request, and profession of faith, Philip there baptized him.

The actual incident of the eunuch's baptism is related in Acts chapter 8, verses 36, 37 and 38:

"And as they went on their way, they came unto a certain water: and the eunuch said, See, here is water; what doth hinder me to be baptized?

"And Philip said, If thou believest with all thine heart, thou mayest. And he answered and said, I believe that Jesus Christ is the Son of God.

"And he commanded the chariot to stand still: and they went down both into the water, both Philip and the eunuch; and he baptized him."

We see here how the practice of the early church was in full accord with the commandments of Christ. Christ said: "He that believeth and is baptized shall be saved." Phillip said to the eunuch: "If thou believest with all thine heart, thou mayest"—be baptized. The eunuch replied: "I believe that Jesus Christ is the Son of God." Thus we see that a person who desires Christian baptism must first be able to confess to faith in Jesus Christ as the Son of God.

A fourth condition for Christian baptism is stated by the apostle Peter in his First Epistle, chapter 3, verse 21. Here Peter is comparing the ordinance of Christian baptism in water to the experience of Noah and his family, who were saved from the wrath and judgment of God as they entered by faith into the ark; and then, once within the ark, passed safely through the waters of the flood. In direct reference to this experience of Noah and his family, Peter says: "The like figure whereunto even baptism doth also now save us (not the putting away of the filth of the flesh, but the answer of a good conscience toward God,) by the resurrection of Jesus Christ."

Here Peter first dismisses the crude suggestion that the purpose of Christian baptism is any kind of cleansing, or bathing, of the physical body. Rather, he says, the essential condition of Christian baptism lies in the inner response of the believer's heart—"the answer of a good conscience toward God." This inner response of a good conscience toward God, Peter indicates, is made possible through faith in the resurrection of Jesus Christ.

We may briefly summarize the grounds upon which the Christian believer at his baptism may answer to God for his conduct with a good conscience. First, such a believer has humbly acknowledged his sins; second, he has confessed his faith in the death and resurrection of Christ as the necessary propitiation for his sins; third, by the outward act of obedience in being baptized he is completing the final requirement of God needed to give him the scriptural assurance of salvation. Having thus met all God's requirements for salvation, he is able to answer God with a good conscience.

We find, then, that there are four main, logical conditions stated in the New Testament for Christian baptism.

The person who is to be baptized must first have been taught enough of the gospel to understand the nature of his act; he must have repented of his sins; he must believe wholeheartedly that Jesus Christ is the Son of God; he must be able to answer God with a good conscience, on the grounds that he has fulfilled all God's requirements for salvation.

We conclude, therefore, that to be eligible for Christian baptism according to the New Testament standard a person must be able to meet these four conditions; and conversely, that any person who is not able to meet these conditions is not eligible for baptism.

It will be seen immediately that these four conditions for baptism automatically rule out one class of persons—and that is infants. By its very nature, an infant cannot be taught, cannot repent, cannot believe, cannot answer with a good conscience to God. Therefore, an infant cannot be eligible for baptism.

Now it is sometimes suggested that there are instances in the New Testament where whole families, or households, were baptized together; and that it is at best probable, if not definitely established, that infant members of these households were included with the rest in the act of baptism. Since this has an important bearing on the whole nature and purpose of baptism, it is desirable to investigate this suggestion with care. The two households usually mentioned in connection with this suggestion are the household of Cornelius, in Acts chapter 10, and the household of the Philippian jailer, in Acts chapter 16.

Let us consider first the household of Cornelius. In Acts chapter 10, verse 2, we are told that Cornelius was "a devout man, and one that feared God with all his house"—that is, all the members of his household were God-fearing people. In verse 33 of the same chapter, Cornelius says to Peter, before the latter begins to preach: "Now therefore are we all here present before God, to hear all things that are commanded thee of God"—this indicates that all those present were capable of hearing Peter's message. In verses 44, 45 and 46 of the same chapter we read how the Holy Spirit fell upon all those present:

"While Peter yet spake these words, the Holy Ghost fell on all them which heard the word.

"And they of the circumcision which believed were astonished, as many as came with Peter, because that on the Gentiles also was poured out the gift of the Holy Ghost.

"For they heard them speak with tongues, and magnify God."

This indicates that all those present were capable not merely of hearing Peter's message, but also of receiving the Holy Spirit by faith, as a result of that message, and of speaking with other tongues. In fact, it was upon this very ground that Peter accepted them as being eligible for baptism, for in the next verses—that is, verses 46 and 47—we read:

"Then answered Peter,

"Can any man forbid water, that these should not be baptized, which have received the Holy Ghost as well as we?"

Futhermore, in the next chapter of Acts—that is, Acts chapter 11—when Peter gives to the apostles and brethren in Jerusalem an account of what had taken place in the house of Cornelius, he adds one further important fact concerning all the members of the household of Cornelius. In Acts chapter 11, verses 12, 13 and 14, Peter gives the following account of how he was received by Cornelius into his house:

"Moreover these six brethren accompanied me, and we entered into the man's house:

"And he shewed us how he had seen an angel in his house, which stood and said unto him, Send men to Joppa, and call for Simon, whose surname is Peter;

"Who shall tell thee words, whereby thou and all thy house shall be saved."

We learn from this that, as a result of Peter's preaching in the house of Cornelius, every member of the household of Cornelius was saved.

If we now put together the various pieces of information that we have gleaned concerning the household of Cornelius, we arrive at the following facts actually stated about them: All of them were God-fearing; all of them heard Peter's message; all of them received the Holy Ghost, and spoke with other tongues; all of them were saved. It is clear therefore that all of these were people capable of meeting the New Testament conditions for baptism; and that there were no infants among them.

Let us now move on to the other instance where the New Testament records the baptism of a whole household at one time. This is recorded in Acts chapter 16. The household is that of the Philippian jailer. As a result of the miraculous earthquake that opened the prison doors and freed Paul and Silas and the other prisoners, the jailer was brought under deep fear and conviction, and desired to know the way of salvation. The incident of the jailer's salvation, and of the baptism of his whole household, is recorded in Acts chapter 16, verses 29 through 34:

"Then he (the jailer) called for a light, and sprang in, and came trembling, and fell down before Paul and Silas,

"And brought them out, and said, Sirs, what must I do to be saved?

"And they said, Believe on the Lord Jesus Christ, and thou shalt be saved, and thy house.

"And they spake unto him the word of the Lord, and to all that were in his house.

"And he took them the same hour of the night, and washed their stripes; and was baptized, he and all his, straightway.

"And when he had brought them into his house, he set meat before them, and rejoiced, believing in God with all his house."

If we study this account carefully, we find that the jailer and the members of his household all shared together in three experiences: In verse 32, we read that Paul and Silas "spake unto him the word of the Lord, and **to all that were in the house**"—that is, all the members of his household heard the message of the gospel. In verse 33, we read that the jailer "was baptized, he and all his, straightway"—that is, all the members of his household were baptized. In verse 34, we read that the jailer "rejoiced, believing in God with all his house"—that is, all the members of his household believed in God.

From this we learn that not merely were all the members of the jailer's household baptized, but all of them also heard and believed the message of the gospel. This shows us that all were capable of meeting personally the New Testament conditions for baptism; and that there were no infants among them.

Neither in the household of Cornelius, nor in the household of the Philippian jailer, nor anywhere else in the New Testament is there any suggestion that infants were ever considered eligible for baptism.

* * *

Although it is most necessary to emphasize the various conditions which those desiring Christian baptism must meet, we must also be careful in this connection to guard against an overemphasis on "teaching", which leads to unscriptural results. In some places—particularly in certain foreign mission fields—it is the established practice to insist that all those who present themselves for baptism be first subjected to a prolonged period of instruction, extending over weeks or months, before they be accepted for baptism. This practice is traced back to the words of Christ in Matthew chapter 28, verse 19: "Go ye therefore, and teach all nations, baptizing them in the name of the Father, and of the Son, and of the Holy Ghost."

Certainly these words show that those desiring to be baptized must be taught first. But the question is: How long does this preliminary process of teaching need to take? Should the time required be measured in months, in weeks, in days, or in hours?

For an answer to this question let us turn briefly to the passages in the New Testament which record the baptism of new converts, and let us accept these passages as our guide.

In Acts chapter 2, verse 41, we read the following conclusion to the events of the day of Pentecost: "Then they that gladly received his word were baptized: and the same day there were added unto them about three thousand souls." The three thousand people whose baptism is here recorded had been a few hours previously open unbelievers, who rejected the claim of Jesus of Nazareth to be either the Messiah of Israel or the Son of God. From the end of Peter's sermon to the moment of their being baptized, the time required by the apostles to give them the necessary instruction could not have exceeded a few hours.

In Acts chapter 8, verse 12, we read the following response of the people of Samaria to the preaching of Philip: "But when they believed Philip preaching the things concerning the kingdom of God, and the name of Jesus Christ, they were baptized, both men and women." No exact period of time for instruction is here specified. As on the day of Pentecost, it could have been just a few hours. Certainly it could not have exceeded a few days, or a week or two at the very most.

A little further on in Acts chapter 8, verses 36 through 39, we read how Philip baptized the Ethiopian eunuch on the very same day that he first met him and preached the gospel to him. Here again, the period could not have exceeded a few hours.

In Acts chapter 9, verses 17 and 18, we read how the disciple Ananias was directed by God to go to Saul of Tarsus and lay hands on him and pray for him. The record here states: "And immediately there fell from his (Saul's) eyes as it had been scales: and he received sight forthwith, and arose, and was baptized." Later, in Acts chapter 22, verse 16, Paul himself relates that Ananias said to him at this time: "And now why tarriest thou? Arise, and be baptized . . ." We see then that Saul of Tarsus—later Paul—was baptized on what was probably the actual day of his conversion—certainly within three days of the first revelation of Jesus Christ to him upon the Damascus road.

In Acts chapter 10, verse 48, we read that Peter commanded Cornelius and his household to be baptized on the same day that he had first preached the gospel to them and the Holy Ghost had fallen upon them all.

In Acts chapter 16, verses 14 and 15, we read how the Lord opened the heart of Lydia, the seller of purple, to the message of the gospel, and how she was then baptized, and all her household. In this case, no further details are given, and no exact period of time is specified.

In Acts chapter 16, verse 33, we read how the Philippian jailer and all his household were baptized the very same night in which they first heard the gospel.

In these passages we have examined seven instances of the baptism of new converts. In all these cases, some measure of instruction was given first. Thereafter, in the majority of these cases, baptism followed within a few hours of conversion. In no case was baptism ever delayed more than a few days.

We are thus able to arrive at a clear picture of the practice of the early church in relation to baptism. Before baptism they presented the simple basic facts of the gospel, centring in the person of Christ, and in His life, death, and resurrection; and they related these facts to the act of baptism.

Baptism then followed immediately—normally, within a few hours—at the most, within a few days.

Finally, after baptism the new converts continued to receive the further, more detailed instruction which was needed to establish them firmly in the Christian faith. This latter phase of instruction is summed up in the verse in Acts chapter 2, which immediately follows the account of the baptism of the new converts—that is, Acts chapter 2, verse 42: "And they—that is, those who had been baptized—continued steadfastly in the apostles' doctrine and fellowship, and in breaking of bread, and in prayers." This is the New Testament pattern for establishing new converts in the faith, after they have been baptized.

IV
Christian Baptism—B

Spiritual Significance Of Baptism: Death And Burial Unto Sin; Resurrection Unto Newness Of Life

Welcome to the Study Hour.

Our textbook—the Bible.

The study which we shall now bring you is No. 20 in our present series, entitled "Foundations."

We are at present working our way systematically through the six great foundation doctrines of the Christian faith, as stated in Hebrews Chapter 6, verses 1 and 2. The six doctrines there listed as the "beginning," or "foundation", of the doctrine of Christ are as follows: No. 1, "repentance from dead works"; No. 2, "faith toward God"; No. 3, "the doctrine of baptisms"; No. 4, "laying on of hands"; No. 5, "resurrection of the dead"; No. 6, "eternal judgment."

In our last three studies we have been examining the third of these great foundation doctrines—that which is called "the doctrine of baptisms."

In the course of these three studies we have hitherto arrived at the following main conclusions:

The plain, literal meaning of the Greek verb, rendered by the word "baptize" in the King James Version, is "to cause something to be dipped, or immersed."

The phrase used in Hebrews chapter 6, verse 2, "the doctrine of baptisms", is plural—"baptisms", not simply "baptism". This agrees with the fact that in the New Testament we find the following four different kinds of baptism mentioned: one, the baptism of John the Baptist; two, the baptism of suffering; three, Christian baptism in water; four, the baptism in the Holy Spirit.

Setting aside the baptism of suffering, as being outside the scope of our present studies, we compared and contrasted the baptism of John the Baptist with full Christian baptism.

We saw that the baptism of John was a special, temporary provision of God, adapted to a transitional period between the dispensation of the law and the prophets and the dispensation of the Christian gospel. The two conditions imposed upon all those who desired John's baptism were that they should confess, and repent of, their sins. Thereafter, the act of being baptized served as a visible seal and assurance that these two conditions had been duly met.

On the other hand, we saw that Christian baptism corresponds to a much greater and fuller spiritual experience. The true Christian believer has not merely confessed and repented of his sins; by faith in Christ's atoning death and resurrection he has been justified, he has received Christ's own righteousness imputed to him by faith. Thereafter, Christian baptism is an outward seal, an outward act of obedience, by which such a believer fulfils, or completes, the inward righteousness which he already enjoys in his heart through faith in Christ.

In line with this, we saw that there are four main logical conditions stated in the New Testament for Christian baptism. The person to be baptized must first have been taught enough of the gospel to understand the nature of his act; he must have repented of his sins; he must believe wholeheartedly that Jesus Christ is the Son of God; he must be able to answer God with a good conscience, on the grounds that he has fulfilled all God's requirements for salvation. Plainly this leaves no room for the baptism of infants, who are unable to fulfil any of these four conditions. On the other hand, we saw that the fulfilling of these conditions does not necessitate, or justify, lengthy periods of elaborate instruction before converts are accepted for baptism. In most of the cases in the New Testament the period required to instruct new converts amounted only to a few hours, and they were normally baptized on the same day that they were converted. Thereafter they went on to receive the further systematic Bible teaching required to establish them firmly in the Christian faith.

*   *   *

In our present study we shall now complete our examination of Christian baptism by unfolding, from the teaching of the New Testament, the true, inward spiritual significance of this ordinance.

The key text, which unlocks the inward spiritual significance of Christian baptism, is found in Romans chapter 6, verses 1 through 7:

"What shall we say then? Shall we continue in sin, that grace may abound?

"God forbid. How shall we, that are dead to sin, live any longer therein?

"Know ye not, that so many of us as were baptized into Jesus Christ were baptized into his death?

"Therefore we are buried with him by baptism into death: that like as Christ was raised up from the dead by the glory of the Father, even so we also should walk in newness of life.

"For if we have been planted together in the likeness of his death, we shall be also in the likeness of his resurrection.

"Knowing this, that our old man is crucified with him, that the body of sin might be destroyed, that henceforth we should not serve sin.

"For he that is dead is freed from sin."

In the previous chapter of Romans—chapter 5—Paul has emphasized the abundance of God's grace towards the depths of man's sin, summed up by the statement in Romans chapter 5, verse 20: "Where sin abounded, grace did much more abound."

This naturally leads on to the question which Paul proceeds to ask in Romans chapter 6, verse 1: "What shall we say then? Shall we continue in sin, that grace may abound?" In other words, Paul imagines someone asking: "If God's grace is in proportion to man's sin, abounding most where sin abounds most, shall we deliberately go on sinning, that God's grace may abound toward us all the more? Is this the way to avail ourselves of God's grace toward sinners?"

Paul's answer to this very dangerous suggestion is that it is based on a complete misunderstanding of the only way in which a sinner can avail himself of God's grace. In order for a sinner to avail himself of God's grace, there must be a definite, personal transaction, by faith, between the sinner and God; and the nature of this transaction is such that it must inevitably produce a total transformation within the personality of the sinner himself. There are two opposite, but mutually complementary, sides to this transformation produced by God's grace in the sinner's personality. First, there is a death—a death to sin, and the old life. Then, there is a new life—a life lived unto God and unto righteousness.

In the light of this fact about the way in which God's grace operates in the sinner, and the results which it produces, we are faced with two alternative, mutually exclusive possibilities: If we have availed ourselves of God's grace, we are, as a necessary consequence, dead to sin; on the other hand, if we are not dead to sin, then we have not availed ourselves of God's grace. It is therefore illogical, and impossible, to speak of availing ourselves of God's grace and at the same time living in sin. These two things can never go together.

Paul himself expresees this fact in Romans chapter 6, verse 2: "God forbid. How shall we, that are dead to sin, live any longer therein?"

Just what we we to understand by this phrase, "dead to sin"? Let us form a picture of what this phrase means, in the following way. Let us imagine the case of a man who has been an outstanding sinner. Let us suppose that he has been habitually unkind and brutal to his wife and childred; he has forbidden all mention of God or of religion in his home; he has used foul and blasphemous language; he has been a slave of liquor and tobacco.

Now let us suppose that this man dies suddenly of a heart attack, sitting in his chair at home. On the table by him there is a lighted cigarette in the ashtray, and a glass of liquor just poured out. Neither the cigarette nor the liquor can any longer produce any reaction from the man; there is no inward stirring of desire, no outward motion of his arm toward them. Why not? The reason is simple: the man is dead—dead to liquor and dead to tobacco alike.

A little later his wife and children come back from the Sunday evening service at the local Gospel Tabernacle, singing the new gospel choruses that they have just learned. There is no reaction from the man—no anger, no violence, no blasphemous words. Why not? The reason is simple: the man is dead—dead to anger and dead to blasphemy alike.

In one short phrase, that man is "dead to sin". Sin no longer has any attraction for him; sin can no longer produce any reaction from him; sin no longer has any power over him.

This is the picture that the New Testament paints of the man who has availed himself, by faith, of God's grace toward the sinner. Through the operation of God's grace, that man has become dead to sin. Sin no longer has any attraction for him; sin can no longer produce any reaction from him; sin no longer has any power over him. Instead, he is alive unto God and unto righteousness.

This fact, that the true Christian believer is, through God's grace, dead to sin, is stated repeatedly and emphatically throughout the New Testament.

For example, it is stated in the verses which we have already read from Romans chapter 6, verses 6 and 7:

"Knowing this, that our old man is crucified with him (Christ), that the body of sin might be destroyed, that henceforth we should not serve sin—that is, not be the slaves of sin.

"For he that is dead is freed—or justified—from sin."

The meaning here is plain: For each person who has accepted the atoning death of Christ on his behalf, the old man—the old corrupt, sinful nature—is crucified; the body of sin has been destroyed; through death, that person has been freed—or justified—from sin. There is no longer any need to serve sin—to be the slave of sin.

A little further on in the same chapter of Romans—chapter 6, verses 11, 12 and 14—Paul repeats this teaching, with renewed emphasis:

"Likewise reckon ye also yourselves to be dead indeed unto sin, but alive unto God through Jesus Christ our Lord.

"Let not sin therefore reign in your mortal body, that ye should obey it in the lusts thereof . . .

"For sin shall not have dominion over you: for ye are not under the law, but under grace."

Again, the meaning is plain: as Christians, we are to reckon ourselves as being dead to sin, through the grace of God in Jesus Christ. As a result, there is no reason why sin should continue to exercise any control or dominion over us.

Further on in the same Epistle to the Romans—chapter 8, verse 10—Paul again states the same truth, in the clearest and most emphatic way: "And if Christ be in you, the body is dead because of sin; but the Spirit is life because of righteousness." The words of Paul here indicate that this truth applies to every true Christian believer in whose heart Christ dwells by faith—"if Christ be in you." The double consequence of Christ indwelling the believer by faith is, first, a death of the old carnal nature—"the body—that is, the body of sin—is dead;" second, a new life unto righteousness through the operation of God's Spirit—"the Spirit is life because of righteousness."

The apostle Peter likewise most clearly presents the same truth, in his First Epistle, chapter 2, verse 24. Speaking of the purpose of Christ's death upon the cross, Peter says: "Who his own self bare our sins in his own body on the tree, that we, being dead to sins, should live unto righteousness." Peter, just like Paul, presents the two complementary aspects of the transformation that takes place within the believer who accepts the atoning death of Christ on his behalf: first, there is a death unto sins; second, there is a life unto righteousness. In fact, Peter states this as being the supreme purpose of Christ's death on the cross—"that we, being dead to sins, should live unto righteousness."

This condition of being dead to sins and alive unto righteousness is something far beyond the mere forgiveness of past sins. In fact, it takes the true believer up into an altogether different realm of spiritual experience. The majority of professing Christians in almost all denominations have some kind of belief that their past sins can be forgiven. In fact, this is probably the main reason why the majority of professing Christians attend church—for the purpose of confessing, and obtaining forgiveness for, the sins which they have committed. However, they have no thought or expectation of experiencing any inward transformation of their own nature. The result is that, having gone through some form of confessing their sins, they leave the church unchanged, to go out and continue committing the same kind of sins that they have been confessing. In due course, they are back in church again, confessing the same sins. This is a man-made religion on the human level, to which some of the outward forms of Christianity have been attached; it has little or nothing in common with the salvation which God offers to the true believer through faith in Christ's atonement.

The central purpose of God in Christ's atonement was not simply that man should be able to receive forgiveness of his past sinful acts; but rather that, once having been forgiven for the past, he should be able to enter into a new realm of spiritual experience—that he should henceforth be dead unto sins, but alive unto God and unto righteousness; that he should no longer be the slave of sin; that sin should no longer have any dominion over him. This has been made possible because Christ, in His atonement, not merely took upon Himself the guilt of our sinful acts and then paid the full penalty for all those acts. Above and beyond this, Christ made Himself one with our corrupt, fallen, sinful nature; and when He died upon the cross, according to the plain statements of scripture, that old nature of ours—"our old man"—"the body of sin"—died in Him, and with Him.

In order that the believer may enter into this, the full purpose of Christ's atonement, there are two simple, but essential conditions that must be fulfilled. These two conditions are stated by Paul, in their logical order, in Romans chapter 6.

In Romans chapter 6, verse 6, Paul says: "Knowing this, that our old man is crucified with him (Christ), that the body of sin might be destroyed, that henceforth we should not serve sin." More literally, "our old man was crucified with him"—that is, it was a single, definite event that occurred at a given moment in past time.

In Romans chapter 6, verse 11, Paul says: "Likewise reckon ye also yourselves to be dead indeed unto sin, but alive unto God through—more literally, in—Jesus Christ our Lord." Here the introductory word "likewise" points out the correspondence between the experience of Christ and the experience of the believer. The meaning is: "Just as Christ died, so reckon that ye also died in Him." More briefly, "Christ's death was your death."

The two conditions for entering into this experience of death unto sin, and of life unto righteousness and unto God, as here stated by Paul, are: first, "knowing"; second, "reckoning". First, we must "know" what God's Word teaches about the central purpose of Christ's death; second, we must "reckon" God's word to be true in our own particular case—we must apply this truth of God's Word by faith to our own condition. The experience can be ours only when, and only as long as, we thus "know", and "reckon" as true, what God's Word teaches about the purpose of Christ's atonement.

Concerning this, the central purpose of Christ's atonement—"that we, being dead to sins, should live unto righteousness"—we may make two statements which can scarcely be challenged: First, there is no truth of greater practical importance than this, contained in the whole revelation of the New Testament; second, there is no truth about which greater ignorance, indifference, or unbelief prevail at the present time among professing Christians. The root of this whole miserable condition lies in the word "ignorance". With good reason we may apply to this situation the words of the Lord in Hosea chapter 4, verse 6: "My people are destroyed for lack of knowledge." The basic condition stated by Paul for entering into the full purpose of Christ's atonement is, "Knowing this . . . " If God's people do not know this truth, they cannot believe it; if they do not believe it, they cannot experience it. Therefore, the first great need is to bring this truth before the church, and to keep it continually before the church, in the clearest and most emphatic way.

Now at this point it may be asked: "What is the relationship between this central truth of Christ's atonement, and the ordinance of Christian baptism?" The answer to this question is very simple, and practical. In the natural realm, after every death there follows a burial. The same order applies also in the spiritual realm: first death, then burial. Through faith in Christ's atonement we reckon ourselves, according to God's Word, to be dead with Him— we reckon our old man, the body of sin, to be dead. Thereafter, the next act appointed by God's word is the burial of this old man, this dead body of sin. The ordinance by which we carry out this burial is the ordinance of Christian baptism. In every service of Christian baptism, carried out according to the pattern of the New Testament, there are two successive stages: first, a burial; second, a resurrection. These two stages of baptism correspond, exactly and perfectly, to the two stages of the inner transformation within the believer who accepts Christ's atonement on his behalf: first, the death unto sin; second, the new life unto righteousness and unto God. Christian baptism in water is, first, a burial in a typical grave of water; and second, a resurrection out of that grave into a new life that is lived unto God and unto righteousness. The burial is the outward expression of the "death unto sin," the "death of the old man"; the resurrection is the outward expression of the new life unto righteousness and unto God.

That this is the true purpose and the true significance of Christian baptism is plainly and emphatically stated in the New Testament.

In Romans chapter 6, verses 3 and 4, we read:

"Know ye not, that so many of us as were baptized into Jesus Christ were baptized into his death?

"Therefore we are buried with him by baptism into death: that like as Christ was raised up from the dead by the glory of the Father, even so we also should walk in newness of life."

Again, in Colossians chapter 2, verse 12, we read:

"Buried with him in baptism, wherein also ye are risen with him through the faith of the operation of God, who hath raised him from the dead."

In both these passages, the two successive stages of baptism are clearly set forth: first, we are buried with Christ by baptism—literally, immersion—into his death; second, we are raised up with him, through faith in the working of God's power, to walk with him in newness of life.

Apart from this basic truth of burial and resurrection, there are three other important facts about baptism contained in these verses:

First, by true Christian baptism we are baptized into Christ Himself—not into any particular church, or sect, or denomination. In agreement with this, Paul says in Galatians, chapter 3, verse 27: "For as many of you as have been baptized **into Christ** have put on Christ." There is no room here for anything less, or smaller, than Christ— Christ in His atoning death, and Christ in His triumphant resurrection.

Second, the effect of baptism depends upon the personal faith of the one being baptized; it is "through the faith of the operation of God"—more simply, "through faith in what God does." Without this faith, the mere ceremony of baptism alone is of no effect or validity whatever.

Third, the believer who is raised up out of the watery grave of baptism to walk in newness of life, does this not in his own power, but in the power of God's glory, the same power that raised Jesus Himself from the grave. In Romans chapter 1, verse 4, Paul says plainly that the power which raised Jesus from the grave was "the Spirit of holiness"—that is, God's own Holy Spirit. Thus the believer who passes through the waters of baptism thereby commits himself to a new life unto God and unto righteousness, which is to be lived in total dependence upon the power of the Holy Spirit. This is in line with what Paul says in Romans chapter 8, verse 10 (the second part): "And if Christ be in you, the body is dead because of sin; but the Spirit is life because of righteousness." God's Spirit alone can give the baptized believer the power that he needs for this new life of righteousness.

It is a general principle of educational psychology that children remember approximately forty percent of what they hear; sixty percent of what they hear and see; eighty percent of what they hear, see and do. In establishing the ordinance of Christian baptism in the church, God has applied this principle of psychology to the teaching of the great central purpose of Christ's atonement—"that we, being dead to sins, should live unto righteousness." According to the New Testament pattern, each time new believers are added to the church, they themselves act out, in the ordinance of baptism, their identification by faith with Christ—first in His death and burial unto sin, second in His resurrection to newness of life. In this way, the ordinance of baptism serves continually to bring and to keep before the whole church the great central purpose of Christ's atonement.

It follows that this great truth concerning Christ's atonement can never be fully restored in the Christian church, until the true method and meaning of Christian baptism are first restored; until Christian baptism becomes once again, for each believer individually, and for the church as a whole, a re-enactment of this double truth— death and burial unto sin, resurrection and life unto righteousness and unto God.

*   *   *

To complete this study, it remains to point out briefly that true Christian baptism does not produce within the believer this condition of "death unto sin", but rather it is the outward seal that the believer has already, by faith, entered into this condition. In the verses already quoted from Romans chapter 6, Paul states clearly that we are first "dead with Christ unto sin"; and then after that we are "baptized into Christ's death".

In this respect, Christian baptism is parallel to John's baptism. In John's baptism, the person to be baptized first repented of his sins, and after that he was "baptized into repentance". In Christian baptism, the believer is first, by faith, dead with Christ unto sin, and after that he is "baptized into Christ's death". In each case the outward act of baptism does not in itself produce the inward spiritual condition; rather, it is the seal and assurance that this inward condition has been produced already, by faith, in the heart of the person baptized.

V

The Baptism In The Holy Spirit—A

Immersion From Above—Drinking Within—The Outward Evidence

Welcome to the Study Hour.

Our textbook—the Bible.

The study which we shall now bring you is No. 21 in our present series, entitled "Foundations".

We are at present working our way systematically through the six great foundation doctrines of the Christian faith, as stated in Hebrews chapter 6, verses 1 and 2. The six doctrines there listed as the "beginning", or "foundation", of the doctrine of Christ are as follows: No. 1, "repentance from dead works"; No. 2, "faith toward God"; No. 3, "the doctrine of baptisms"; No. 4, "laying on of hands"; No. 5, "resurrection of the dead"; No. 6, "eternal judgment".

In our last four studies we have been examining the third of these great foundation doctrines—that which is called "the doctrine of baptisms".

We pointed out that the plural form of the word "**baptisms**" indicates that more than one kind of baptism is referred to; and we discovered that the New Testament does in fact speak in various places of four different types of baptism. These are as follows: first, the baptism of John the Baptist; second, the baptism of suffering; third, Christian baptism in water; fourth, the baptism in the Holy Spirit.

Setting aside the baptism of suffering, as being outside the scope of our present studies, we examined and compared, in turn, the baptism of John the Baptist and Christian baptism in water.

In order to complete this study in "the doctrine of baptisms", it now remains for us to examine the fourth type of baptism spoken of in the New Testament—that is, "the baptism in the Holy Spirit".

It will be helpful to begin by summarizing briefly certain conclusions which we formed as to the general meaning of the word "baptism".

First, we saw that, by linguistic origin and usage alike, the Greek verb rendered in the King James Version "to baptize" has one definite, well-established, unchanging meaning: "to cause something to be dipped, or immersed."

Second, we saw that there are two features of baptism, as described in the New Testament, which are common to each of the four types of baptism there described. In each case, baptism is, by its nature, first, total; and second, transitional. It is total, in the sense that it involves the whole person and the whole personality of the one being baptized; it is transitional, in the sense that in each case the person being baptized passes out of one stage, or realm of experience, into a new stage, or realm, of experience, from which there is afterwards no way of return back to the previous stage.

It will be helpful to bear in mind these general features of baptism as unfolded in the New Testament, as we turn now to the particular examination of the fourth type of baptism—"the baptism in the Holy Spirit".

During the past fifty years or so, this subject—the baptism in the Holy Spirit—has been arousing keen interest and discussion amongst ever widening circles of the Christian church. Today it is, without doubt, a theme of study, of discussion, and quite often of controversy, in almost all sections of Christendom. In view of this, we shall seek to approach this study in a way that is careful, thorough, and scriptural.

* * *

First we shall enumerate the passages in the New Testament where the word "baptize" is used in connection with the Holy Spirit. Appropriately enough—since "seven" is distinctively the number of the Holy Spirit—there are seven such passages, and they are as follows:

In Matthew chapter 3, verse 11, John the Baptist contrasts his own ministry with the ministry of Christ which is to follow, and he uses these words: "I indeed baptize you with water unto repentance: but he that cometh after me is mightier than I, whose shoes I am not worthy to bear: he shall baptize you with the Holy Ghost, and with fire." (We must add that, although the King James Version here uses the English preposition "with" in conjunction with the verb "to baptize", the actual preposition used in the original Greek is the preposition "in". This applies equally to baptizing in water and to baptizing in the Holy Ghost. In each case, the Greek preposition used is "in". In fact, the only prepositions ever used anywhere in the New Testament in conjunction with the verb "to baptize" are the prepositions "in" and "into". In the original Greek text, no other prepositions are ever joined with the verb "to baptize". It is unfortunate that the King James Version has, by using a variety of different prepositional forms, obscured the clear teaching of the original text).

In Mark chapter 1, verse 8, the words of John the Baptist concerning Christ are rendered as follows: "I indeed have baptized you with water: but he shall baptize you with the Holy Ghost." (In each case, the Greek preposition used is "in".)

In Luke chapter 3, verse 16, the words of John the Baptist are rendered as follows: "John answered, saying unto them all, I indeed baptize you with water; but one mightier than I cometh, the latchet of whose shoes I am not worthy to unloose: he shall baptize you with the Holy Ghost and with fire." (Here again, the literal translation is "in the Holy Ghost".)

In John chapter 1, verse 33, the testimony of John the Baptist concerning Christ is given as follows: "And I knew him not: but he that sent me to baptize with water, the same said unto me, Upon whom thou shalt see the Spirit descending, and remaining on him, the same is he which baptizeth with the Holy Ghost." (Again, in each case the Greek preposition used is "in".)

In Acts chapter 1, verse 5, shortly before His ascension into heaven, Jesus says to His disciples: "For John truly baptized with water; but ye shall be baptized with the Holy Ghost not many days hence." (More literally, Jesus says: "Ye shall be baptized in the Holy Ghost.")

In Acts chapter 11, verse 16, Peter is describing the events which took place in the household of Cornelius, and in this connection he quotes the actual words of Jesus as given in Acts chapter 1, verse 5, for he says: "Then remembered I the word of the Lord, how that he said, John indeed baptized with water; but ye shall be baptized with the Holy Ghost."

Finally, in First Corinthians chapter 12, verse 13, Paul says: "For by one Spirit are we all baptized into one body, whether we be Jews or Gentiles, whether we be bond or free; and have been all made to drink into one Spirit." (Here the King James Version uses the preposition "by"— "by one Spirit are we all baptized into one body." However, the preposition used in the original Greek text is the preposition "in"—"in one Spirit are we all baptized into one body." Thus, the usage of Paul in this passage is in perfect harmony with the usage of the Gospels and the book of Acts.) Unfortunately, the accident that the King James translators used the phrase "by one Spirit" in this particular passage has given rise to some strange doctrines which suggest that Paul is here referring to some special experience, different from that referred to in the Gospels or the book of Acts, and that in this special experience the Holy Spirit is himself the agent who does the baptizing. Had the authors of these doctrines paused long enough to consult the original Greek text, they would have found no basis or suggestion there of any such doctrine. In fact, the whole teaching of the entire New Testament in this connection agrees in this fact, clearly and emphatically stated: Jesus Christ Himself alone—and no other—is the One who baptizes in the Holy Ghost.

We must also add that Paul's usage here of the phrase "to baptize into", in connection with the baptism in the Holy Spirit, agrees with the usage of the same phrase which we have already noted in connection with John's baptism and with Christian baptism in water. In both these cases we pointed out that the act of baptism was an outward seal and assurance of an inward spiritual condition into which the person being baptized had already entered by faith. The same applies to Paul's statement here about the relationship between the baptism in the Holy Spirit and membership of the body of Christ. The baptism in the Holy Spirit does not constitute a person a member of the body of Christ. Rather, it is a supernatural seal, acknowledging that that person has already become a member of Christ's body by faith.

Let us now briefly summarize the lessons which we may learn from considering the above seven passages in the New Testament where the phrase "to baptize in the Holy Spirit" is used:

In six out of these seven passages, the experience of being baptized in the Holy Spirit is both compared, and contrasted, with being baptized in water.

In two out of the seven passages, "fire" is joined with "the Holy Spirit", and the experience is described as "being baptized in the Holy Spirit and fire."

Apart from the verb "to baptize", the only other verb used in these passages in connection with the Holy Spirit is the verb "to drink". In First Corinthians chapter 12, verse 13, Paul says: "We have been all made to drink into one Spirit." In modern English we should say, more simply: "We have been all given to drink of one Spirit."

The use of the verb "to drink" agrees with what Jesus Himself says concerning the Holy Spirit, in John chapter 7, verses 37, 38 and 39:

"Jesus stood and cried, saying, If any man thirst, let him come unto me, and **drink**.

"He that believeth on me, as the scripture hath said, out of his belly shall flow rivers of living water.

"(But this spake he of the Spirit, which they that believe on him should receive: for the Holy Ghost was not yet given; because that Jesus was not yet glorified.)"

Here Jesus speaks plainly of an experience in which the believer is to receive the gift of the Holy Spirit through a process analogous to that of drinking in water.

This in turn harmonizes with the passage in Acts chapter 2, verse 4, concerning the disciples in the upper room on the day of Pentecost, where it states that "they were all filled with the Holy Ghost."

It agrees also with various passages in the book of Acts which speak about believers "receiving the Holy Ghost." For example, in Acts chapter 8, verses 15 and 17, concerning the Samaritans converted through the preaching of Philip, we read that the apostles Peter and John were later sent down to them from Jerusalem: "who, when they were come down, prayed for them, that they might **receive** the Holy Ghost . . . Then laid they their hands on them, and they **received** the Holy Ghost."

Again, in Acts chapter 10, verse 47, Peter says concerning the people in the house of Cornelius upon whom the Holy Spirit had just fallen: "Can any man forbid water, that these should not be baptized, which have **received** the Holy Ghost as well as we?"

Further on, in Acts chapter 19, verse 2, Paul asks the disciples whom he meets at Ephesus: "Have ye **received** the Holy Ghost since ye believed?"

In all these passages, the use of phrases such as "to drink in of the Holy Spirit," "to be filled with the Holy Spirit," "to receive the Holy Spirit," suggests an experience in which the believer receives the fulness of the Holy Spirit inwardly within himself.

On the other hand, we have seen that the literal, root meaning of the verb "to baptize" is "to cause something to be dipped, or immersed." Thus, the phrase "to be baptized in the Holy Spirit" suggests an experience in which the believer's whole personality is immersed, surrounded, enveloped in the presence and power of the Holy Spirit, coming down over him from above and from without.

In full accord with this aspect of the experience, we find that, without exception, in every place in the book of Acts where the baptism in the Holy Spirit is described, language is used which clearly suggests that the Holy Spirit comes down over, or is poured out upon, the believer from above.

For example, in Acts chapter 2, verse 2, we read that on the day of Pentecost "there came a sound from heaven as of a rushing mighty wind, and it **filled all the house** where they were sitting." These words clearly reveal that the Holy Spirit came down over these disciples from above and completely immersed and enveloped them, even to the extent of filling the whole house where they were sitting. Further on in the same chapter, Peter twice confirms this interpretation of the experience. In Acts chapter 2, verse 17, he declares that this experience is the fulfilment of God's promise: "In the last days . . . I will **pour out** of my Spirit upon all flesh . . ." And in verse 33, he says again concerning Christ: "Therefore being by the right hand of God exalted, and having received of the Father the promise of the Holy Ghost, he hath **shed forth** this, which ye now see and hear." The Greek word here translated "shed forth" is the same as that which in verse 17 is translated "pour out". In each case the picture is clearly one of the Holy Spirit coming down over the believer from above.

In Acts chapter 8, verse 16, the phrase used for the same experience is that of the Holy Ghost "falling upon" the believers. Here again, the picture is clearly one of the Spirit coming down over them from above.

In Acts chapter 10, concerning the people in the house of Cornelius, both phrases are used one after the other. In verse 44 we read: "the Holy Ghost **fell on** all them which heard the word." In verse 45 we read: "on the Gentiles also was **poured out** the gift of the Holy Ghost." This shows that the phrases "to fall upon" and "to be poured out upon" are used interchangeably in this connection.

Again, in Acts chapter 11, verse 15, Peter describes the same event in the house of Cornelius, and says: "the Holy Ghost **fell on** them as on us at the beginning." Here the phrase, "as on us at the beginning", indicates that the experience of Cornelius and his household is in this respect exactly parallel to the experience of the disciples in the upper room on the day of Pentecost.

Finally, in Acts chapter 19, verse 6, we read concerning the disciples in Ephesus, after they had been baptized in water: "And when Paul laid his hands upon them, the Holy Ghost **came on** them . . ." Here the phrase "to come on" is obviously similar in meaning to the phrase used in previous passages, "to fall upon".

If we now seek to fit together the pictures, or impressions, created by the various phrases which we have found used in the New Testament, we arrive at a conclusion which may be briefly summarized as follows:

The experience of which we are speaking is made up of two distinct, but complementary aspects, one outward, and the other inward.

Outwardly, the invisible, but absolutely real, presence and power of the Holy Spirit come down from above upon the believer, and completely surround, envelope, and immerse him.

Inwardly, the believer, in the likeness of one drinking, receives the presence and power of the Holy Spirit within himself, until there comes a point at which the Holy Spirit, thus received, in turn wells up within the believer and flows forth like a river from within the inmost depths of his being.

No human language can fully exhaust the various phases and aspects of a mighty, supernatural experience such as this, but it may perhaps be illuminating to borrow a picture from the Old Testament. In the days of Noah we read that the whole world that then existed was submerged beneath the flood. In bringing about this flood, we read that God used two distinct, but complementary processes. In Genesis chapter 7, verse 11, we read the following account of how the flood was brought about: "In the six hundredth year of Noah's life, in the second month, the seventeenth day of the month, the same day were all the fountains of the great deep broken up, and the windows of heaven were opened."

This account reveals that the waters of the flood came from two sources: from within, "the fountains of the great deep were broken up"; from above, "the windows of heaven were opened," and the rain was poured down.

We must of course observe that the flood of Noah's day was a flood of divine wrath and judgment; the flood into which the New Testament believer is plunged is a flood of divine mercy, and glory, and blessing. However, with this qualification, the experience of the New Testament believer, who receives the fulness of the Holy Spirit, exhibits the same two aspects as in the account of the flood: from within, the fountains of the great deep within the believer's own personality are broken up and there gushes out a mighty flood of blessing and power from within him; from above, the windows of God's mercy are opened upon the believer, and from these opened windows there is poured upon him such a deluge of glory and blessing that his whole personality is immersed in its outpourings.

It must be emphasized that we are not here speaking of two separate experiences, but rather of two distinct, yet complementary aspects which together make up the fulness of one single experience.

Someone may object that it is difficult to understand how the believer can at one and the same time be filled with the Holy Spirit from within, and immersed in the Holy Spirit from without. However, such an objection in reality serves only to illustrate the limitations of human speech and understanding. An exactly similar type of objection might be brought against such statements as those made by Christ Himself, that He is in the Father and the Father in Him; or again, that Christ is in the believer, and the believer in Christ.

In the last resort, if men persist in cavilling at a supernatural experience of this kind on the basis of human limitations of expression or understanding, the best and shortest answer is found in the words of the Scottish preacher, who said: "It's better felt, than telt!"

* * *

Up to this point we have considered the inward, invisible nature of the baptism in the Holy Spirit, as revealed by the words used in the New Testament to describe it. We must now go on to consider what are the outward manifestations which accompany this inward experience.

First of all, we must point out that it is perfectly scriptural to use the word "manifestation" in connection with the Holy Spirit. We acknowledge of course that the Holy

Spirit Himself is, by His very nature, invisible. In this respect, He is compared by Jesus to the wind. In John chapter 3, verse 8, Jesus says concerning the operation of the Holy Spirit: "The wind bloweth where it listeth, and thou hearest the sound thereof, but canst not tell whence it cometh, and whither it goeth: so is every one that is born of the Spirit." Although the wind itself is invisible, the effects which the wind produces, when it blows, can in many cases be both seen and heard. For example, when the wind blows, the dust rises from the streets; the trees all bend in one direction; the leaves rustle; the waves of the sea roar; the clouds go flying across the sky. These effects produced by the wind can be seen, or heard.

So it is, Jesus says, with the Holy Spirit. The Spirit Himself is invisible. But the effects which the Holy Spirit produces, when He begins to work, can often be seen, or heard. This fact is confirmed by the language used by the New Testament in various places.

For example, in Acts chapter 2, verse 33, the apostle Peter refers to the effects produced by the descent of the Holy Spirit on the day of Pentecost, and he says: "Therefore being by the right hand of God exalted, and having received of the Father the promise of the Holy Ghost, he (Christ) hath shed forth this, which ye now **see and hear.**" Here "this" refers to the effects of the Holy Spirit at work, which, Peter says, can be both seen and heard.

Again, in First Corinthians, chapter 2, verse 4, Paul describes his own ministry in these words: "My speech and my preaching was not with enticing words of man's wisdom, but in **demonstration** of the Spirit (that is, the Holy Spirit) and of power." Further on in the same Epistle —First Corinthians, chapter 12, verse 7—Paul says: "The **manifestation** of the Spirit is given to every man to profit withal." Notice the phrases which Paul uses in connection with the Holy Spirit—"the demonstration of the Spirit," and "the manifestation of the Spirit." These two words "demonstration" and "manifestation" show clearly that the presence and operation of the Holy Spirit can produce effects which can be directly perceived by the physical senses.

With this in mind, let us now turn to the various passages in the New Testament where the baptism in the Holy Spirit is described—that is, where we are told what actually happened to the people who received this experience—and let us see what are the outward manifestations which accompany this operation of the Spirit.

There are actually three places in the New Testament where we are told what happened when people were baptized in the Holy Spirit. These three places are: Acts chapter 2, verses 2, 3 and 4; Acts chapter 10, verses 44, 45 and 46; and Acts chapter 19, verse 6.

We shall consider, in order, the actual words used in each of these three passages to describe what took place.

First, Acts chapter 2, verses 2, 3 and 4. This is the record of what happened to the first disciples on the day of Pentecost:

"And suddenly there came a sound from heaven as of a rushing mighty wind, and it filled all the house where they were sitting.

"And there appeared unto them cloven tongues like as of fire, and it sat upon each of them.

"And they were all filled with the Holy Ghost, and began to speak with other tongues, as the Spirit gave them utterance."

Second, Acts chapter 10, verses 44, 45 and 46. This is the record of what happened when Peter first preached the gospel to Cornelius and his household:

"While Peter yet spake these words, the Holy Ghost fell on all them which heard the word.

"And they of the circumcision which believed were astonished, as many as came with Peter, because that on the Gentiles also was poured out the gift of the Holy Ghost.

"For they heard them speak with tongues, and magnify God."

Third, Acts chapter 19, verse 6. This describes what happened to the first group of converts, to whom Paul preached at Ephesus:

"And when Paul had laid his hands upon them, the

Holy Ghost came on them; and they spake with tongues, and prophesied."

If we now carefully compare these three passages, we shall find that there is one—and only one—outward manifestation which is common to all three occasions where people received the baptism in the Holy Spirit. In each case, the scripture clearly states that those who received this experience "spoke with tongues"—or "spoke with other tongues."

Other supernatural manifestations are also mentioned, but none are mentioned as having taken place on more than one of the three occasions.

For example, on the day of Pentecost there was the sound of a rushing wind, and visible tongues of fire were seen. However, these manifestations were not repeated on the other two occasions.

Again, at Ephesus we read that the new converts not only spoke with tongues, but also prophesied. However, this manifestation of prophesying is not mentioned as having taken place either on the day of Pentecost or in the house of Cornelius.

The only manifestation which is common to all three occasions is that all those who received the experience "spoke with tongues."

The apostle Peter and the other Jews, who already knew what had taken place on the day of Pentecost, went to the house of Cornelius reluctantly, against their own inclinations, under the explicit direction of God. At that time the Jewish Christians did not believe that the gospel was for the Gentiles, or that Gentiles could be saved and become Christians. However, the moment that Peter and the other Jews heard the Gentiles speak with tongues, they immediately understood and acknowledged that these Gentiles had received the Holy Spirit just as truly and as fully as the Jews themselves. They never asked for any other evidence beside this. The scripture says that "they were astonished, because that on the Gentiles also was poured out the gift of the Holy Ghost. For they heard them speak with tongues . . ." For Peter and the other

Jews, the sole and sufficient evidence that the Gentiles had received the Holy Spirit was that they had heard them speak with tongues.

In the next chapter of Acts—Acts chapter 11—we read that Peter was called to account by the other leaders of the church in Jerusalem for his conduct in visiting and preaching to Gentiles. In his own defence, he explained what had taken place in the house of Cornelius. In this connection, he says, in Acts chapter 11, verse 15: "And as I began to speak, the Holy Ghost fell on them, as on us at the beginning." Thus Peter directly compares the experience which the household of Cornelius received with that which the first disciples received on the day of Pentecost—for he says, "as on us at the beginning." Yet in the house of Cornelius there was no mention of a mighty rushing wind, or tongues of fire. The one sufficient manifestation which set the apostolic seal upon the experience of Cornelius and his household was that they spoke with tongues.

From this we conclude that the manifestation of speaking with tongues, as the Holy Spirit gives utterance, is the accepted New Testament evidence that a person has received the baptism in the Holy Spirit. In confirmation of this conclusion, we may make the following statements:

First, this was the evidence which the apostles themselves received in their own experience.

Second, this was the evidence which the apostles themselves accepted in the experience of others.

Third, the apostles never asked for any other alternative evidence.

Fourth, no other alternative evidence is offered to us anywhere in the New Testament.

In our next study in this series, we shall examine this conclusion further; and we shall consider various criticisms, or objections, which are commonly raised against it.

VI
The Baptism In The Holy Spirit—B

A Distinct Experience From Salvation—The Teaching
Of Jesus—Dwelling With And Dwelling In

Welcome to the Study Hour.

Our textbook—the Bible.

The study which we shall now bring you is No. 22 in our present series, entitled "Foundations".

We are at present working our way systematically through the six great foundation doctrines of the Christian faith, as stated in Hebrews chapter 6, verses 1 and 2. The six doctrines there listed as the "beginning", or "foundation", of the doctrine of Christ are as follows: No. 1, "repentance from dead works"; No. 2, "faith toward God"; No. 3, "the doctrine of baptisms"; No. 4, "laying on of hands"; No. 5, "resurrection of the dead"; No. 6, "eternal judgment".

We are at present examining the third of these great foundation doctrines—that which is called "the doctrine of baptisms".

Having examined in succession the baptism of John the Baptist and Christian baptism in water, we commenced in our last study to examine the last remaining type of baptism described in the New Testament—that which is called "the baptism in the Holy Spirit".

First of all, we considered what is the actual nature of this experience itself, as revealed in the New Testament, and we saw that the experience has two distinct, but complementary, aspects—one outward, and the other inward.

Outwardly, the invisible, but absolutely real, presence and power of the Holy Spirit come down from above upon the believer, and completely surround, envelope, and immerse him.

Inwardly, the believer, in the likeness of one drinking, receives the presence and power of the Holy Spirit within himself, until there comes a point at which the Holy Spirit, thus received, in turn wells up within the believer and flows forth like a river from within the inmost depths of his being.

After considering the actual nature of the experience itself, we then went on to consider what outward manifestation can be accepted as evidence, according to the New Testament, that a person has been baptized in the Holy Spirit. We examined the three passages in the New Testament where we are told what actually happened to people who received the baptism in the Spirit, and we formed the conclusion that the manifestation of speaking with tongues, as the Holy Spirit gives utterance, is the accepted New Testament evidence that a person has been baptized in the Holy Spirit.

In confirmation of this conclusion, we put forward the following statements:

First, this was the evidence which the apostles themselves received in their own experience.

Second, this was the evidence which the apostles themselves accepted in the experience of others.

Third, the apostles never asked for any other alternative evidence.

Fourth, no other alternative evidence is offered to us anywhere in the New Testament.

Now a number of different objections are often raised against this conclusion that the manifestation of speaking with tongues is the accepted New Testament evidence that a person has received the baptism in the Holy Spirit. For the sake of clarity and thoroughness, therefore, it is necessary for us to consider a number of the most common objections to this conclusion.

One of the commonest objections takes the following form: Every Christian who has had a genuine experience of conversion and salvation has automatically received the Holy Spirit in that experience, and therefore does not need any further experience, or any other evidence, in order to have the assurance of having received the Holy Spirit.

In considering this objection, we are naturally led to ask whether the teaching on which it is based is true and scriptural. Can we assert, on the basis of the New Testament, that every Christian, who has had a genuine experience of conversion and salvation, has, in virtue of that experience, necessarily thereby received the Holy Spirit?

The best way to answer this question is to consider the examples of people in the New Testament who had quite clearly been converted and become real Christians; and to see whether the New Testament teaches that these people had, because of that experience, necessarily received the Holy Spirit.

The first example that we shall consider is that of the apostles themselves. Let us consider the apostles as they were in the period between the resurrection of Jesus and His ascension into heaven. At this time the apostles had repented of their sins, and had forsaken all to follow Jesus; they believed that Jesus was the Christ (the Messiah); they had personally witnessed, and accepted as true, the facts of His death, burial, and resurrection. In John chapter 20, verse 22, we read that, when Jesus first appeared to His disciples together, after His resurrection, "he breathed on them, and saith unto them, Receive ye the Holy Ghost." The scripture does not reveal exactly what took place within the apostles at this moment, when Jesus breathed upon them. Certainly it would seem absolutely unreasonable to deny that, from that time forward—if not previously—the apostles were, in the fullest sense, genuine, converted Christians. Nevertheless, it is perfectly plain that their experience of the Holy Spirit was still incomplete. The proof of this is that, in His final words to them before His ascension into heaven, Jesus commanded them not to go out and preach immediately, but to go back to Jerusalem and to wait there until they should be baptized in the Holy Spirit and should thus be endued with power from on high for effective witness and service.

In Luke chapter 24, verse 49, Jesus says to them: "And, behold, I send the promise of my Father upon you: but tarry ye in the city of Jerusalem, until ye be endued with power from on high."

In Acts chapter 1, verse 5, the words of Jesus to the apostles are recorded as follows: "For John truly baptized with water; but ye shall be baptized with the Holy Ghost not many days hence." And again, in Acts chapter 1, verse 8: "But ye shall receive power, after that the Holy Ghost is come upon you: and ye shall be witnesses unto me . . . "

This promised experience of being baptized in the Holy Ghost and of being endued with power from on high to witness for Christ came to the apostles on the day of Pentecost. It is recorded in Acts chapter 2, verse 4: "And they were all filled with the Holy Ghost, and began to speak with other tongues, as the Spirit gave them utterance."

Taken in its proper context, this verse shows plainly that, although the apostles were already genuine, converted Christians, it was not until the day of Pentecost that they were actually filled with, or baptized in, the Holy Spirit. Here, then, is one scriptural example which indicates that it is possible for people to have been converted and to have become genuine Christians, but not yet to have been filled with, or baptized in, the Holy Spirit.

Let us now consider the example of the people of Samaria, as recorded in Acts chapter 8. In Acts chapter 8, verse 5, we read: "Then Philip went down to the city of Samaria, and preached Christ unto them." Further on in the same chapter—Acts chapter 8, verse 12—we read concerning these same people: "But when they believed Philip preaching the things concerning the kingdom of God, and the name of Jesus Christ, they were baptized, both men and women." These people had now heard the truth of Christ preached to them by Philip; they had believed; they had been baptized. It would be unreasonable and unscriptural to deny that these people were saved.

In Mark chapter 16, verses 15 and 16, we read Christ's own commission to the apostles to preach the gospel: "And he said unto them, Go ye into all the world, and preach the gospel to every creature. He that believeth and is baptized shall be saved; but he that believeth not shall be damned."

The people of Samaria had heard the gospel preached; they had believed and they had been baptized. Therefore we know, on the authority of Christ's own words, that they were saved. Yet these same people up to this time had not received the Holy Spirit. This is made absolutely clear as we read on further in Acts chapter 8, verses 14 through 17:

"Now when the apostles which were at Jerusalem heard that Samaria had received the word of God, they sent unto them Peter and John:

"Who, when they were come down, prayed for them, that they might receive the Holy Ghost:

"(For as yet he was fallen upon none of them: only they were baptized in the name of the Lord Jesus.)

"Then laid they their hands on them, and they received the Holy Ghost."

We see that the people of Samaria received salvation through the ministry of Philip; they received the Holy Spirit through the ministry of Peter and John. Their receiving the Holy Spirit was a separate experience, subsequent to their receiving salvation. Here, then, is a second scriptural example which indicates that it is possible for people to have been converted and to have become genuine Christians, but not yet to have received the Holy Spirit.

In this connection it is interesting to notice that, in the passage in Acts chapter 8, we find two different forms of speech used. One speaks of "receiving the Holy Spirit"; the other speaks of "the Holy Spirit falling upon them". However, the context makes it absolutely plain that these are not two different experiences, but two different aspects of one and the same experience.

This agrees with the various forms of speech which are used in connection with the outpouring of the Holy Spirit upon the household of Cornelius. In Acts chapter 10, verses 44 through 47, we find the following three different phrases all used to describe the same experience: "The Holy Ghost fell on them"; "the gift of the Holy Ghost was poured out on them"; "they received the Holy Ghost". Again, in Acts chapter 11, verses 15 through 17, when the apostle Peter describes the same incident, we find the following three phrases used: "The Holy Ghost fell on them"; they were "baptized with the Holy Ghost"; "God gave them the gift" of the Holy Ghost.

Putting these passages together, we find that, in all, a total of five different phrases are used to describe one and the same experience. These five phrases are as follows: "the Holy Ghost fell on them"; "the gift of the Holy Ghost was poured out on them"; "they received the Holy Ghost"; they were "baptized with the Holy Ghost"; "God gave them the gift" of the Holy Ghost. A number of modern interpreters would suggest that these various different phrases refer to various different experiences. However, this is definitely not in line with the usage of the apostles in the New Testament. According to the apostles, these different phrases all denote one single experience. It is the same thing for a person to receive the Holy Ghost, or to receive the gift of the Holy Ghost, as it is for that person to be baptized in the Holy Ghost, or for the Holy Ghost to be poured out upon that person, or for the Holy Ghost to fall upon that person.

Let us now turn on to Acts chapter 19, verses 1 through 6. This passage describes how Paul came to Ephesus and met there certain people who are described as "disciples". The first question that Paul asked these people was: "Have ye received the Holy Ghost since ye believed?" It is plain that Paul had been given the impression that these people were disciples of Christ. Obviously, if they were not Christians at all, there could have been no question of their having received the Holy Ghost, since this is received only through faith in Christ. However, through further questioning, Paul discovered that these people were not disciples of Christ at all, but only of John the Baptist, and so he then went on to preach to them the gospel of Christ.

One fact emerges clearly from this incident so far. Obviously, if people always received the Holy Ghost automatically, as an immediate consequence of believing in Christ, it would be illogical and foolish for Paul to ask the question: "Have ye received the Holy Ghost **since ye believed?**" The mere fact that Paul asked this question makes it clear that he recognized the possibility of people having become disciples, or believers in Christ, without having received the Holy Ghost.

This is confirmed by the record of events which follows in the next few verses. After Paul had explained the gospel of Christ to these people, we read, in Acts chapter 19, verse 5: "When they heard this, they were baptized in the name of the Lord Jesus." These people had now heard and believed the gospel, and they had been baptized. As we have already shown in connection with the people of Samaria, on the authority of Christ's own words, people who have fulfilled the two conditions of believing and being baptized are thereby saved. Nevertheless, these people in Ephesus, just like those in Samaria, had not yet received the Holy Spirit. In Ephesus, just as in Samaria, this came as a separate and subsequent experience; and it is described in the next verse—Acts chapter 19, verse 6: "And when Paul had laid his hands upon them, the Holy Ghost came on them; and they spake with tongues, and prophesied."

Here then, in the case of these people at Ephesus, is a third scriptural example which indicates that it is possible for people to have been converted, and to have become genuine Christians, but not yet to have received the Holy Spirit. This conclusion drawn from the record of the book of Acts is further confirmed by what Paul himself says in his Epistle to the Ephesians. We must bear in mind that this group of disciples whom Paul met and ministered to in Ephesus were among the Ephesian Christians to whom Paul later wrote his epistle. In this Epistle to the Ephesians, chapter 1, verse 13, Paul reminds these people of the successive stages in which they were originally converted and received the Holy Ghost. Speaking of their coming to believe in Christ, Paul says: "In whom ye also trusted, after that ye heard the word of truth, the gospel of your salvation: in whom also after that ye believed, ye were sealed with that Holy Spirit of promise." Here Paul indicates that there were three separate, successive stages in their experience: first, they heard the gospel; second, they trusted, or believed, in Christ; third, they were sealed with the Holy Spirit. This agrees exactly with the historical record in Acts chapter 19, which states that these people first heard the gospel; then they believed, and were baptized: finally, when Paul thereafter laid his hands upon them, the Holy Ghost came on them. In both accounts alike—in Acts and in Ephesians—it is absolutely clear that these people received the Holy Spirit, not simultaneously with conversion, but as a separate and subsequent experience, after conversion.

For a fourth example, of a different kind, we shall now turn back for a few moments to Acts chapter 10, verses 34 through 48. This passage records the sermon which Peter preached in the house of Cornelius, and the results which followed his preaching. The scripture here seems to indicate that as soon as Cornelius and his household heard the gospel and put their faith in Christ, they immediately received the Holy Spirit and spoke with tongues. However, we must add that, although in this instance these two experiences happened together, they still remain two quite distinct experiences. Furthermore, the evidence that Cornelius and his household had received the Holy Spirit, was not the fact that they had put their faith in Christ, but the fact that, under the impulse of the Holy Spirit, they spoke with tongues.

We have now carefully considered, in all, four different groups of people found in the New Testament; first, the apostles; second, the people of Samaria; third, the disciples at Ephesus; fourth, Cornelius and his household. Of these four groups, we have seen clearly that the first three— the apostles, the people of Samaria, the disciples at Ephesus—had all been converted and become Christians, **before** they received the Holy Spirit. Their receiving the Holy Spirit was a separate and subsequent experience, following after their conversion.

In the case of the fourth group—Cornelius and his household—it would appear that these people received the Holy Spirit at the same time as they put their faith in Christ. However, even in this instance, their receiving the Holy Spirit was a distinct experience from their believing in Christ; and it was openly attested by the fact that they spoke with tongues. A careful examination of the whole of the rest of the New Testament would seem to show that there is no other instance recorded, apart from Cornelius and his household, in which people received the Holy Spirit ·at the same time as they believed in Christ. We are therefore justified in concluding that, in this respect, the experience of Cornelius and his household is the exception, rather than the rule.

On the basis of this careful examination of the New Testament record, we may now set forth the following conclusions.

First, it is normal for a Christian to receive the Holy Spirit as a separate and subsequent experience, following after conversion.

Second, even if a person receives the Holy Spirit at the same time as conversion, receiving the Holy Spirit still remains, logically, a quite distinct experience from being converted.

Third, whether a person receives the Holy Spirit at the same time as conversion, or following after conversion, the evidence that that person has received the Holy Spirit still remains the same: the person speaks with tongues, as the Holy Spirit gives utterance.

Fourth—as a logical consequence of the foregoing—the fact that a person has been genuinely converted and has become a real Christian, does not by itself constitute evidence that that person has received the Holy Spirit.

This conclusion concerning the relationship between conversion and receiving the Holy Spirit has been based mainly on a study of the book of Acts. However, it is in full accord with the teaching of Jesus Himself on this same topic in the gospels.

For example, in Luke chapter 11, verse 13, Jesus says to His disciples: "If ye then, being evil, know how to give good gifts unto your children: how much more shall your heavenly Father **give the Holy Spirit** to them that ask Him?" The teaching of this verse—reinforced by the examples, which precede it, of a son asking his father successively for bread, for a fish, and for an egg—is clearly to the effect that God, as a heavenly Father, is willing to give the Holy Spirit to His believing children, if they will ask for it. However, a person must first be converted and put his faith in Christ, in order to become a child of God. Plainly, therefore, Jesus teaches not that the Holy Spirit is received at conversion, but rather that it is a gift which every converted child of God thereafter has a right to ask for, as a son from his Father. Furthermore, Jesus here definitely places an obligation upon the children of God to ask their heavenly Father specifically for this gift of the Holy Spirit. It is therefore not scriptural for a Christian to assume, or to assert, that he automatically received the gift of the Holy Spirit at conversion, without asking for it.

Again, in John chapter 7, verse 38, Christ says: "He that believeth on me, as the scripture hath said, out of his belly shall flow rivers of living water." In the first half of the next verse these "rivers of living water" are interpreted by the writer of the gospel as referring to the Holy Spirit, for he says: "But this spake he of the Spirit, which they that believe on him should receive . . . " In both these verses it is made plain that the gift of the Holy Spirit, bringing forth rivers of living water from within, is to be received by those who are already believers in Christ. It is something which they should go on to receive, after believing in Christ.

Christ teaches the same truth again in John chapter 14, verses 15, 16 and 17, where He says:

"If ye love me, keep my commandments.

"And I will pray the Father, and he shall give you another Comforter, that he may abide with you forever;

"Even the Spirit of truth; whom the world cannot receive, because it seeth him not, neither knoweth him: but ye know him; for he dwelleth with you, and shall be in you."

In this passage, "the Comforter" and "the Spirit of truth" are two different designations of the Holy Spirit. Christ teaches here plainly that the gift of the Holy Spirit is not for the unbelieving people of this world, but for Christ's own disciples who love and obey Him. This confirms therefore that it is the privilege of God's believing children, Christ's disciples, to go on to receive the gift of the Holy Spirit, as they meet God's conditions.

Furthermore, in this passage Jesus indicates two different possible relationships between the Holy Spirit and the believer. He says: "He dwelleth with you, and shall be in you." At this time, it is clear, the Holy Spirit was already dwelling with the disciples, but He was not yet dwelling in them. In the experience of the disciples, the transition from the first to the second relationship took place on the day of Pentecost, when they were baptized in the Holy Ghost. Thereafter, each of them knew the Holy Spirit as an indwelling personal presence, and no longer merely as a companion, teacher, and guide.

So it is with each born-again Christian. The Holy Spirit dwells with him. Such a person is no stranger to the Holy Spirit. Obviously this is so, for without the influence of the Holy Spirit a person cannot be convicted of sin, cannot repent, cannot believe in Christ, cannot be born again. All these are operations of the Holy Spirit. However, the fact that a person has received all these experiences is not by itself evidence that the Holy Spirit dwells in that person. Such a person is in the same condition as the disciples before the day of Pentecost: the Holy Spirit dwells with him, but not yet in him. To receive the Holy Spirit as an indwelling personal presence and power is a separate and subsequent experience. It is the privilege and the responsibility of each believer to go on to seek and to receive this experience personally.

According to the patterns and principles of the New Testament, the evidence that a believer has received this baptism in the Holy Spirit is that he speaks with other tongues, as the Spirit gives him utterance.

In our next study we shall consider some further objections, or misunderstandings, which commonly arise in connection with the scriptural doctrine of speaking with tongues.

VII
The Baptism In The Holy Spirit—C

Do All Speak With Tongues?—Is There Any Other Evidence?

Welcome to the Study Hour.

Our textbook—the Bible.

The study which we shall now bring you is No. 23 in our present series, entitled "Foundations".

We are at present working our way systematically through the six great foundation doctrines of the Christian faith, as stated in Hebrews chapter 6, verses 1 and 2. In our last six studies we have been considering the third of the six doctrines there listed—that which is called "the doctrine of baptisms".

Having examined in succession the baptism of John the Baptist and Christian baptism in water, we are now engaged in examining the last remaining type of baptism described in the New Testament—that which is called "the baptism in the Holy Spirit".

Concerning this, we have hitherto reached two main conclusions.

First, the experience itself has two distinct, but complementary aspects—one outward, and the other inward. Outwardly, the invisible, but absolutely real, presence and power of the Holy Spirit come down from above upon the believer, and completely surround, envelope, and immerse him. Inwardly, the believer, in the likeness of one drinking, receives the presence and power of the Holy Spirit within himself, until there comes a point at which the Holy Spirit, thus received, in turn wells up within the believer and flows forth like a river from within the inmost depths of his being.

Secondly, we concluded that the manifestation of speaking with tongues, as the Holy Spirit gives utterance, is the accepted New Testament evidence that a person has received the baptism in the Holy Spirit.

We then went on to consider an objection that is commonly raised against speaking with other tongues as the evidence of having received the baptism in the Holy Spirit. This objection states that every Christian, who has had a genuine experience of conversion and salvation, has automatically received the Holy Spirit in that experience, and therefore does not need any further experience, or any other evidence, in order to have the assurance of having received the Holy Spirit.

In considering this objection, we were led to examine the cases of a number of different groups of people in the New Testament who are known to have received the baptism in the Holy Spirit. As a result, we could find only one example in the whole of the New Testament where people apparently received the baptism in the Holy Spirit at the same time as they were converted. This group of people was Cornelius and his household. In every other case in the New Testament where evidence is available, we discovered that people were converted first, and then received the baptism in the Holy Spirit as a separate and subsequent experience, accompanied by the manifestation of speaking with other tongues. Even in the case of Cornelius and his household, the evidence that they had received the Holy Spirit was just the same as in all the other cases which are described—that is, they were heard to speak with other tongues. Thus, our careful and thorough examination of all these cases served only to confirm our conclusion that the manifestation of speaking with other tongues is the accepted New Testament evidence that a person has received the baptism in the Holy Spirit.

*   *   *

We shall now go on to consider some other objections, or misunderstandings, which commonly arise in connection with this doctrine of speaking in tongues.

One common such objection, or misunderstanding, is based on the words of the apostle Paul in First Corinthians, chapter 12, verse 30, where he asks: "Do all speak with tongues?" A careful examination of the context shows that Paul clearly implies that the answer to his question is "No"—"all do not speak with tongues."

Does this mean, then, that there were Christians in the New Testament church who had received the baptism in the Holy Spirit without speaking with tongues? No, this is not what Paul is saying. A careful examination of the whole passage reveals that Paul is not here speaking about the experience of being baptized in the Holy Spirit, but about various possible ministries, or supernatural manifestations, of the Spirit, which can be exercised by the believer in the church, subsequent to, and as a result of, the initial experience of being baptized in the Holy Spirit.

Let us look at what Paul says two verses previously, in First Corinthians cahpter 12, verses 27 and 28:

"Now ye are the body of Christ, and members in particular.

"And God hath set some in the church, first apostles, secondarily prophets, thirdly teachers, after that miracles, then gifts of healings, helps, governments, diversities of tongues."

Paul is here speaking of various different ministries or gifts of the Holy Spirit, which may be exercised by different members within the church. Amongst these he enumerates "diversities of tongues". In the margin of the King James Version the alternative translation given for this is "kinds of tongues"—and this is, in fact, the correct literal translation.

Exactly the same expression is used by Paul still earlier in the same chapter. In First Corinthians chapter 12, verses 7 through 11, Paul enumerates nine different possible gifts, or manifestations, of the Holy Spirit, which may be granted to believers who have been baptized in the Holy Spirit. The list which he enumerates is as follows:

"But the manifestation of the Spirit is given to every man to profit withal.

"For to one is given by the Spirit the word of wisdom; to another the word of knowledge by the same Spirit;

"To another faith by the same Spirit; to another the gifts of healing by the same Spirit;

"To another the working of miracles; to another prophecy; to another discerning of spirits; to another divers kinds of tongues; to another the interpretation of tongues:

"But all these worketh that one and the selfsame Spirit, dividing to every man severally as he will."

That Paul is here speaking about manifestations or gifts of the Spirit that are found in the experience of believers subsequent to their receiving the initial baptism in the Spirit, is made plain by what Paul says two verses further on—that is, in First Corinthians chapter 12, verse 13: "For by one Spirit are we all baptized into one body . . . " Or, more literally, and more clearly: "For in one Spirit we were all baptized into one body . . . " We see therefore that Paul here speaks of the baptism in the Spirit as an experience that has already been received in the past; and that the nine gifts, or manifestations, of the Spirit, which he lists here, are found in the experience of believers subsequent to, and as a result of, their having initially been baptized in the Holy Spirit. Paul indicates that though the initial baptism in the Holy Spirit is for all believers—"in one Spirit were we all baptized into one body"—thereafter the various gifts, or manifestations, of the Spirit are divided up amongst believers according to the sovereign will of the Spirit Himself, with the result that one believer may receive one gift, and another believer may receive another gift.

Among the nine gifts, or manifestations, of the Spirit here listed by Paul, we find that the eighth in the list is "divers kinds of tongues". The word "divers" has been put in by the translators. The actual phrase in the original Greek is simply "kinds of tongues". It is therefore identical in the original with the phrase translated in First Corinthians chapter 12, verse 28, "diversities of tongues". This makes it plain that in both these passages Paul is talking about one and the same thing—namely, that particular gift or manifestation of the Holy Spirit which is called in the original text "kinds of tongues". It is outside the scope of our present study to examine in detail the exact nature or operation of this particular gift. It is sufficient for our present purposes to have established the fact that in the passages which we are considering Paul is talking not about the initial experience of being baptized in the Holy Spirit, but about one of the nine distinct gifts of the Spirit which can be manifested in the experience of a believer as a result of his having first received the initial baptism in the Spirit.

From this it follows that, in First Corinthians chapter 12, verse 30, when Paul says "Do all speak with tongues?", the question which he has in mind is not: "Have all at one time spoken in tongues?"—that is, when they were initially baptized in the Holy Spirit. On the contrary, the question with which he is now concerned is this: "Do all believers, who have been baptized in the Holy Spirit, thereafter regularly exercise the gift of tongues?" To this question the answer—both then, and now—is a definite "No." In many different sections of the Christian church today—as doubtless also in the original New Testament church—there are believers who have received the baptism in the Holy Spirit with the New Testament evidence of speaking in tongues, but who thereafter never regularly exercise the gift of tongues. In this respect, therefore, the experience of modern believers after being baptized in the Spirit is in full accord with the examples and teachings of the New Testament.

We may perhaps sum up the experience of such believers as these by saying that they have received the gift of the Holy Spirit, but they have not received the gift of tongues—more exactly, "kinds of tongues". These people have been baptized in the Holy Spirit—they have received the indwelling Spirit in His personal fulness—but thereafter they do not normally, or regularly, manifest that particular one of the nine supernatural gifts, or manifestations, of the Holy Spirit, which the New Testament calls "kinds of tongues".

This distinction between the initial gift of the Holy Spirit Himself, accompanied with the manifestation of speaking in tongues, and the subsequent gift of "kinds of tongues", is very carefully preserved by the linguistic usage of the New Testament. The Greek word used in the New Testament for "gift", when it denotes the gift of the

Holy Spirit Himself, received at the baptism in the Spirit, is always the word *"dorea"*. The Greek word for "gift", when it denotes any of the nine different gifts, or manifestations, of the Spirit (including the gift of tongues) is the word *"charisma"*. These two words are never interchanged anywhere in the New Testament. *"Charisma"* is never used to denote the gift of the Holy Spirit Himself, initially received at the baptism in the Spirit. Conversely, *"dorea"* is never used to denote any of the nine separate and subsequent gifts, or manifestations, of the Holy Spirit, found in the lives of believers who have already received the baptism in the Holy Spirit. The language, the teaching, and the examples of the New Testament all alike indicate a clear distinction between these two aspects of spiritual experience.

* * *

Those who teach that speaking with tongues is not necessarily the evidence of having received the baptism in the Holy Spirit are obliged by logic to suggest some alternative form of evidence by which we may know, according to scripture, that a person has received the baptism in the Holy Spirit.

One such form of alternative evidence which is quite commonly proposed is that of spiritual fruit. The teaching is that unless a person demonstrates in his life the fruit of the Holy Spirit in a very clear and full way, then that person cannot be considered to have received the baptism in the Holy Spirit.

The complete list of the fruit of the Holy Spirit is given by Paul in Galatians, chapter 5, verses 22 and 23:

"But the fruit of the Spirit is love, joy, peace, longsuffering, gentleness, goodness, faith, meekness, temperance."

This, and other passages, make it plain that the primary form of the fruit of the Spirit, out of which all the rest develop, is "love".

Now only a very foolish and shallow-minded Christian would ever deny that spiritual fruit in general, and love in particular, are of the greatest possible importance in the life of every Christian. However, this does not mean that spiritual fruit can be accepted as the scriptural evidence of having received the baptism in the Holy Spirit. In fact, this test of spiritual fruit must be rejected as being contrary to scripture on two main grounds: first, it is not the test which the apostles themselves applied; second, it overlooks the clear, scriptural distinction between a gift and fruit.

Let us consider first the test which the apostles applied. When the first disciples on the day of Pentecost received the baptism in the Holy Spirit, with the outward manifestation of speaking with other tongues, the apostle Peter did not wait several weeks or months to see whether this experience would produce in the lives of himself and the other disciples a much greater measure of spiritual fruit than they had previously enjoyed. On the contrary, he stood up the very same hour, and said without any doubts or qualifications: "This is that which was spoken by the prophet Joel; And it shall come to pass in the last days, saith God, I will pour out of my Spirit upon all flesh . . . "

What evidence did Peter have for making this statement? Nothing but the fact that they all began to speak with other tongues. No further evidence besides this was required.

Again, in Acts chapter 8, we read that after many people in Samaria had been converted through the preaching of Philip, the apostles Peter and John then went down to pray for them that they might receive the Holy Ghost. The record of what took place is given in Acts chapter 8, verses 14 through 20:

"Now when the apostles which were at Jerusalem heard that Samaria had received the word of God, they sent unto them Peter and John:

"Who, when they were come down, prayed for them, that they might receive the Holy Ghost:

"(For as yet he was fallen upon none of them: only they were baptized in the name of the Lord Jesus.)

"Then laid they their hands on them, and they received the Holy Ghost.

"And when Simon saw that through laying on of the apostles' hands the Holy Ghost was given, he offered them money,

"Saying, Give me also this power, that on whomsoever I lay hands, he may receive the Holy Ghost.

"But Peter said unto him, Thy money perish with thee, because thou hast thought that the gift of God may be purchased with money."

From this account we understand that these people in Samaria had only been converted for a matter of a few days, or at the most a few weeks. Yet they received the Holy Ghost through the laying on of the apostles' hands as one single experience. Thereafter there was no question of waiting to see whether in the course of the ensuing weeks and months sufficient spiritual fruit would be manifested in the lives of these new converts to prove that they really had received the Holy Spirit. No, their receiving the Holy Spirit was one single, definite experience, after which no further evidence or tests were needed.

In this connection it is sometimes objected that the scripture does not explicitly state that these people in Samaria spoke with tongues when they received the Holy Spirit. This is quite true. However, the scripture does make it plain that, through the laying on of the apostles' hands, there was an open demonstration of supernatural power such that Simon, who had been a professional sorcerer, was willing to pay money in order that he might receive the power to produce a similar supernatural demonstration in any people upon whom he in turn might thereafter lay his hands.

If we accept that these people in Samaria, as a result of the laying on of the apostles' hands, spoke with other tongues as the Holy Spirit gave them utterance, this will fit in with every detail of the story as it is recorded in the book of Acts, and it will also bring the case of the people in Samaria into line with the cases of all the other people in the book of Acts who are known to have received the baptism in the Holy Spirit.

On the other hand, if people prefer to assume that in

this particular incident in Samaria there was some other supernatural manifestation, which was not speaking with tongues, they must at least acknowledge that we have no way whatever of finding out what form this other kind of supernatural manifestation may have taken. Upon this assumption, therefore, it is not possible to build any kind of positive doctrinal conclusion concerning the baptism in the Holy Spirit. For example, a person cannot say: "I have not spoken with tongues; nevertheless, I know that I have received the baptism in the Holy Spirit because I have received the same evidence, or experience, as the people of Samaria." If the people of Samaria did not speak with tongues, there is no way of knowing what else they may have done instead. Thus, this assumption that the people of Samaria did not speak with tongues leads only to conclusions which are completely negative and sterile, and which do not in any way affect the positive conclusions which we have been able to form from the other cases where we do know that people, on receiving the baptism in the Spirit, did speak with tongues.

Another case which is sometimes brought forward in this connection is that of the apostle Paul, as related in Acts chapter 9. This decisive incident of Paul's conversion, and the events which accompanied it, is related in Acts chapter 9, verses 17 and 18:

"And Ananias went his way, and entered into the house; and putting his hands upon him said, Brother Saul, the Lord, even Jesus, that appeared unto thee in the way as thou camest, hath sent me, that thou mightest receive thy sight, and be filled with the Holy Ghost.

"And immediately there fell from his eyes as it had been scales: and he received sight forthwith, and arose, and was baptized."

Surely if there was ever a case where the early church might justifiably have applied the test of fruit, it was in the case of Saul of Tarsus, now become Paul. Up to that time Paul had been, on his own admission, the bitterest opponent of the gospel and persecutor of the church. Yet here we now find him receiving the Holy Spirit, in a single experience, through the laying on of the hands of Ananias, and thereafter there is not the faintest suggestion that any further test of fruit in his life may have to be applied.

Once again, in this case of Paul, there are those who object that the scripture does not state that Paul spoke with tongues when Ananias laid hands on him. It is true that the scripture here gives no details whatever of what happened to Paul. However, side by side with this account in Acts chapter 9, we must set Paul's own personal testimony in First Corinthians chapter 14, verse 18, where he says: "I thank my God, I speak with tongues more than ye all." When we combine this testimony of Paul's with the other examples given in the book of Acts, it becomes only natural and reasonable to conclude that Paul first began to speak with tongues when Ananias laid his hands upon him that he might be filled with the Spirit. This conclusion is further strengthened by the subsequent record of Acts, that when Paul himself later laid his hands upon new converts, they in turn spoke with tongues. This is recorded of the new converts at Ephesus, in Acts chapter 19, verse 6: "And when Paul had laid his hands upon them, the Holy Ghost came on them; and they spake with tongues, and prophesied." It would be quite unnatural to suppose that Paul laid his hands upon these converts in order to transmit to them an experience which he had never received himself.

One further, and decisive, case is that of Cornelius and his household, as related in Acts chapter 10. Peter and the other believing Jews went to the house of Cornelius with reluctance, against their own inclinations, only because God had explicitly directed them to go. After Peter had been preaching a short while, the Holy Spirit fell upon all who heard his word. Peter and the other Jews were amazed, because they heard these Gentiles speaking with tongues. Up to this very moment Peter, like other Jewish Christians, had not believed that it was possible for Gentiles, such as Cornelius, to be saved and become Christians. Yet this one manifestation of speaking with tongues immediately convinced Peter and the other Jews that these Gentiles were now just as much Christians as the Jews themselves. Peter never suggested that it would be necessary to subject these Gentiles to any further tests, or to look for spiritual fruit, or any other kind of evidence, in their lives. On the contrary, he immediately commanded that they be baptized, by which act they were openly accepted and attested as full Christians.

In Acts chapter 11, verses 15 and 17, we read the account of this incident which Peter later gave to the other leaders of the apostolic church in Jerusalem. He says:

"And as I began to speak, the Holy Ghost fell on them, as on us at the beginning . . .

"Forasmuch then as God gave them the like gift as he did unto us, who believed on the Lord Jesus Christ; what was I, that I could withstand God?"

We know from the previous chapter that Cornelius and his household all spoke with tongues. Yet in this account here Peter does not find it necessary to mention this decisive manifestation. He merely says: "The Holy Ghost fell on them, as on us at the beginning . . . God gave them the like gift as he did unto us . . ." In other words, the manifestation of speaking with tongues was at this time so universally accepted as the evidence of receiving the Holy Spirit, that Peter did not even need to mention it. Both he, and the other church leaders, took this manifestation for granted.

The conclusion of the other church leaders is stated in the next verse—Acts chapter 11, verse 18: "When they heard these things, they held their peace, and glorified God, saying, Then hath God also to the Gentiles granted repentance unto life."

What convinced Peter and the other apostles that Gentiles could experience salvation through faith in Christ just as fully as Jews? One thing, and one thing only: the fact that they heard these Gentiles speak with tongues. In the whole of this account there is never any suggestion that Peter or any other of the apostles ever looked for any other kind of evidence in these Gentiles' lives, apart from the fact that they spoke with tongues. There was no question of waiting for spiritual fruit to be manifested.

In this, the apostles were perfectly logical. Not because fruit is unimportant, but because fruit is, by its very nature, totally different from a gift. A gift is received by a single act of faith; fruit is produced by a slow, gradual process, which includes planting, tending, and cultivating.

The baptism in the Holy Spirit is a gift—a single experience—received by faith. The evidence that a person has received this gift is that he speaks with other tongues. Thereafter, one main purpose for the which the gift is given is that it may enable the person to produce more and better spiritual fruit than he could ever otherwise have produced. It is no error to emphasize the importance of fruit. The error consists in confusing a gift with fruit, in confusing the evidence that a gift has been received with the purpose for which the gift has been given.

In our next study we shall go on to consider a number of other common misunderstandings connected with tongues as the evidence of having received the baptism in the Holy Spirit.

VIII
The Baptism In The Holy Spirit—D

*The Place Of Emotion—Physical Reactions—Three Principles
Confirming The Evidence Of Tongues*

Welcome to the Study Hour.

Our textbook—the Bible.

The study which we shall now bring you is No. 24 in our present series, entitled "Foundations".

We are at present considering that part of Christian doctrine which is called, in Hebrews chapter 6, verse 2, "the doctrine of baptisms".

Under this heading we examined, first, the baptism of John the Baptist; then, Christian baptism in water; and now we are engaged in examining the last remaining type of baptism described in the New Testament—that which is called "the baptism in the Holy Spirit".

We saw that this experience has two aspects—one outward, and the other inward. Outwardly, the believer is immersed in the presence and power of the Holy Spirit, coming down over him from above. This outward aspect of the experience explains the use of the word "baptism" in this connection. Inwardly, the believer receives the presence and power of the Holy Spirit within himself, until there comes a point at which the Holy Spirit, thus received, in turn wells up within the believer and flows forth like a river from within the inmost depths of his being. This inward aspect of the experience explains why the scripture compares the receiving of the Holy Spirit to the act of drinking.

We then went on to consider what is the scriptural evidence by which we may know that a person has received this experience of being filled with, or being baptized in, the Holy Spirit; and we came to the conclusion that the manifestation of speaking with other tongues, as the Holy Spirit gives utterance, is the accepted New Testament evidence that a person has received the baptism in the Holy Spirit.

We took note of the fact that a number of objections are commonly raised against tongues as the evidence of having received the Holy Spirit: such as that a truly converted Christian necessarily has received the Holy Spirit, and therefore needs no further evidence, or experience; or, alternatively, that there may be other scriptural forms of evidence, apart from speaking with tongues, which prove that a person has received the Holy Spirit.

We considered each of these objections carefully in turn, but we found that none of them could be substantiated by a thorough examination of all the relevant passages of scripture.

We shall now go on to consider some further objections, or misunderstandings, which commonly arise in connection with speaking in tongues as the evidence of the baptism in the Holy Spirit.

One view which is commonly held today is that the baptism in the Holy Spirit is, first and foremost, an intense emotional experiencè. One word with strong emotional associations quite often used in this connection is the word "ecstasy". This view of the baptism in the Holy Spirit would seem to draw its support mainly from two sources. First, there are some theologians, who do not actually have the experience themselves, but who theorize about it on the basis of passages in the New Testament or in the writings of the early Church Fathers. For some reason or other, these theologians seem to have chosen the word "ecstasy", or "ecstatic", as a good theological sounding word, with which to sum up the essential nature of this supernatural experience. Secondly, there are many believers who have actually received the experience, and who, by a common tendency of human nature, when testifying of it to others, lay the main emphasis on their own subjective, emotional reactions to the experience. The result is that they convey to those who hear them, often without meaning to do so, the impression that the essential nature of the experience is emotional. Probably the particular emotion most commonly mentioned in this connection is that of "joy".

Now, in considering the relationship between the emotions and the baptism in the Holy Spirit, we do well to begin by acknowledging two important facts.

First, man is an emotional creature. His emotions constitute an integral and important part of his total make-up. Therefore, man's emotions have an important part to play in his total worship and service of God. True conversion neither suppresses nor obliterates a man's emotions. True conversion, on the contrary, first liberates, and then redirects, a man's emotions. If a man's emotions have not entered into his total experience of conversion—if they have not been brought under the control and the power of the Holy Spirit, then that man is not yet fully converted.

Secondly, we must also acknowledge that the word "joy" is often, in scripture, closely associated with the Holy Spirit. For instance, the fruit of the Spirit, as listed in Galatians chapter 5, verse 22, is first "love", then "joy", and so on. In this list, "joy" comes second, immediately after love itself, which is the primary form of the fruit of the Spirit. Again, we read, in Acts chapter 13, verse 52, concerning the early Christians in the city of Antioch: "And the disciples were filled with joy, and with the Holy Ghost." Thus we see that, in the New Testament, joy is often closely associated with the Holy Spirit.

Nevertheless, the teaching that intense joy, or any other strong emotion, by itself constitutes evidence of the baptism in the Holy Spirit, cannot be reconciled with the New Testament. For this, there are two main reasons.

First, in the actual passages where the baptism in the Holy Spirit is described, there is never any direct mention whatever of emotion in any form. Never once is any form of emotion mentioned, either as the evidence, or as the direct consequence, of having received the Holy Spirit. Any person who bases his doctrine of receiving the Holy Spirit on any emotional experience has no scriptural basis for his doctrine. This fact is quite contrary to the thinking of the natural man, and usually surprises the average religious person who does not base his thinking directly on the New Testament. In fact, it sometimes happens that believers, seeking the Holy Spirit, receive a clear, scriptural experience of speaking with other tongues exactly as recorded in the New Testament, and yet they are afterwards unconvinced and dissatisfied with their experience, simply because they were not conscious of any intense or wonderful emotion, such as they had wrongly been led to expect.

We may illustrate this by the example of a little boy who asks his parents for a spaniel puppy as a birthday present. When the present arrives, it is a beautiful golden cocker spaniel puppy, exhibiting all the marks of a real pedigree spaniel of its class. Nevertheless, to the parents' dismay, the little boy who receives this gift is obviously far from satisfied with it. When his parents seek the reason for his dissatisfaction, they discover that all the little fellow's friends have been telling him for weeks past that all spaniels are always black, and therefore he has formed in advance the most strong expectation that the puppy which he is to receive will be black. No matter how beautiful the golden puppy may be, it cannot now satisfy him, simply because it fails to live up to his expectation of being black. Yet his opinion that all spaniels are black has no basis at all in fact, but has been formed merely by listening to the opinions of friends his own age, who know no more about spaniels than he himself.

So it is sometimes with Christians who ask their heavenly Father for the gift of the Holy Spirit. In answer to their prayer they receive an experience of speaking with other tongues which is in perfect accord with the examples and the teaching of the New Testament. Yet they are not satisfied with this scriptural answer to their prayers, simply because it did not happen to be marked by any intense emotional experience. They fail to realize that their anticipation of some intense emotion was based in the first instance on the ill-considered opinions of misguided fellow Christians, not on the clear teaching of the New Testament.

The second reason why we cannot accept any strong emotion, like joy, as evidence of receiving the Holy Spirit is that there are instances in the New Testament of believers who experienced a wonderful sense of joy, but who nevertheless had not yet received the Holy Spirit. For instance, we read in Luke, chapter 24, verses 52 and 53, concerning the first disciples, after the ascension of Jesus, but before the day of Pentecost:

"And they worshipped him, and returned to Jerusalem with great joy:

"And were continually in the temple, praising and blessing God. Amen."

Here we find that the disciples, even before the day of Pentecost, experienced great joy in their worship of God. Nevertheless, we know that it was not until the day of Pentecost itself that they were actually baptized in the Holy Ghost.

Again, we read in Acts chapter 8, verse 8, the following description of the city of Samaria, after the people of the city had heard and believed the gospel of Christ, preached to them by Philip: "And there was great joy in that city."

We see that the whole-hearted acceptance of the gospel immediately brought great joy to these people. Nevertheless, as we read on in the same chapter, we discover that it was only later, through the ministry of Peter and John, that these people received the Holy Spirit.

These two examples of the first disciples, and of the people of Samaria, prove, therefore, that an intense emotional experience, such as great joy, is not an essential part of the baptism in the Holy Spirit, and cannot be accepted as evidence of having received this baptism.

Another type of experience often associated by some people with the baptism in the Holy Spirit is some kind of very powerful physical sensation in their body. Over the course of years I have had occasion to question many people as to the grounds on which they based their claim to have received the baptism in the Holy Spirit, and I have found that people often associate this experience with some very strong physical sensation, or reaction. The following are some of the experiences which have actually been mentioned to me, in this connection, at various times: a sensation as of a very powerful electric current; a sensation as of a fire, or of intense heat in some other form; being prostrated forcefully on the floor; a powerful shaking of the whole body; seeing a very bright light; hearing the actual voice of God speaking; having a vision of heavenly glories; and so on.

Once again, in considering theories of this kind, we must acknowledge that they contain an important element of truth. Throughout the course of the Bible we find many instances where the immediate presence and power of almighty God produced strong physical reactions in the bodies of those of His people who were counted worthy to come thus close to Him.

In Genesis chapter 17, verses 1 through 3, we read that when the Lord appeared to Abraham and began to speak to him, Abraham fell upon his face. Several times in the books of Leviticus and Numbers we read that when God's presence and glory were visibly manifested among His people, both Moses and Aaron and others also of the children of Israel fell upon their faces. In First Kings chapter 18, verse 39, we read that, when the fire fell upon Elijah's sacrifice and all the people saw it, they fell upon their faces. In Second Chronicles chapter 5, verses 13 and 14, we read, concerning the dedication of Solomon's temple: "Then the house was filled with a cloud, even the house of the Lord; so that the priests could not stand to minister by reason of the cloud: for the glory of the Lord had filled the house of God."

There are two passages in which the prophet Jeremiah gives his own personal testimony of the strong physical effects produced within him by the power of God's Word and God's presence.

In Jeremiah chapter 20, verse 9, he says:

"Then I said, I will not make mention of him, (that is, of the Lord), nor speak any more in his name. But his word was in mine heart as a burning fire shut up in my bones, and I was weary with forbearing, and I could not stay." Here Jeremiah testifies that the prophetic message of the Lord within his heart produced the impression of a burning fire in his bones.

A little further on, in Jeremiah chapter 23, verse 9, he says again:

"Mine heart within me is broken because of the prophets; all my bones shake; I am like a drunken man, and like a man whom wine hath overcome, because of the Lord (more literally, from the face, or presence, of the Lord), and because of the words of his holiness." Here also, Jeremiah's words indicate plainly a most powerful physical reaction to God's presence.

Again, in Daniel chapter 10, verses 7 and 8, we read of the powerful physical effects produced upon Daniel and his companions by a direct vision of the Lord.

"And I Daniel alone saw the vision: for the men that were with me saw not the vision: but a great quaking (or trembling) fell upon them, so that they fled to hid themselves.

"Therefore I was left alone, and saw this great vision, and there remained no strength in me: for my comeliness (or my physical vigour) was turned in me into corruption, and I retained no strength."

At the immediate presence of the Lord, Daniel and his companions—just like Jeremiah—experienced strong and unusual physical reactions.

. Nor are reactions of this kind confined only to the Old Testament. In Acts chapter 9, verses 3 through 6, we read of the vision of the Lord granted to Saul of Tarsus on his way to Damascus. This account indicates that Saul saw a very bright light; he heard a voice speaking to him from heaven; he fell to the earth; and his body trembled.

Again, in Revelation chapter 1, verses 10 through 17, we read of a vision of the Lord granted to the apostle John on the island of Patmos. After recording this vision, John says: "And when I saw him, I fell at his feet as dead." Here again, there was obviously a very powerful and dramatic physical reaction to the immediate presence of the Lord.

In some of the older established denominations of the Christian church there is a tendency to dismiss all such physical reactions or manifestations as these, with labels such as "emotionalism", or "fanaticism". However, this attitude plainly goes far beyond what scripture warrants. Doubtless, there can be occasions when manifestations of this kind are the product of "emotionalism", or "fanaticism"—or, more probably, of a carnal desire for self-display. But who would dare to bring charges such as these against men like the prophets Moses, Jeremiah and Daniel, or the apostles John and Paul? Too often the tendency to reject all forms of physical reaction to the presence and power of God is based on false, man-made traditions of what constitutes true holiness, or of the kind of behaviour that is acceptable to God in the worship of His people.

We see, then, that the scripture gives room for various forms of powerful, or unusual, reactions in the bodies of God's people, caused by special experiences of His immediate presence, or power. However, nowhere does the scripture ever suggest that any of the physical reactions, or manifestations, such as we have mentioned, could ever constitute evidence that a person has received the baptism in the Holy Spirit. In the case of the Old Testament prophets, such as Moses, or Jeremiah, or Daniel, we know that none of these received the baptism in the Holy Spirit, because this experience was never granted to anyone before the day of Pentecost.

Again, in the cases of John and Paul in the New Testament, we know that the strong physical reactions which they experienced to the presence of the Lord were not evidence of their receiving the baptism in the Spirit. In the case of John on Patmos, at the time when he received this vision, he had already been baptized in the Holy Spirit more than fifty years previously. In the case of Paul on the road to Damascus, none of the physical reactions which he experienced there constituted evidence that he had received the Holy Spirit. It was three days later, in the city of Damascus itself, when Ananias laid hands upon him, that Paul first was filled with the Holy Spirit.

No matter from what angle we may approach this subject, we are always brought to the same conclusion: There is one, and only one, physical manifestation which constitutes evidence that a person has received the Holy Spirit. That manifestation is speaking with other tongues, as the Spirit gives utterance.

* * *

In closing this study, let us mention briefly three different, but basic, principles of scripture, all of which confirm that speaking with other tongues is the appropriate evidence that a person has received the Holy Spirit.

In Matthew chapter 12, verse 34, Jesus says: "Out of the abundance of the heart the mouth speaketh." In other words, the heart of man, when it is filled to overflowing, overflows through the mouth. This applies to the baptism in the Holy Spirit. When a person's heart has been filled to overflowing with the Holy Spirit, the overflow of the heart then takes place through the mouth. Because the infilling is supernatural, the overflow is supernatural also. The person speaks a language which he has never learned and does not understand, using this to glorify God.

Again, in James chapter 3, verse 8, we read: "But the tongue can no man tame (or control); it is an unruly evil, full of deadly poison." And in Romans chapter 6, verse 13, the scripture commands us: "Yield yourselves unto God, as those that are alive from the dead, and your members as instruments of righteousness unto God." God here demands more than the mere yielding of our wills—that is, of ourselves. He demands that we actually yield to him our physical members, that He may control them according to His own will as instruments of righteousness. The final evidence, or seal, that this yielding of our physical members to God has been made complete is that the Spirit of God takes control of the very member which none of us can control for ourselves—that is, the tongue—and then uses this member in a supernatural way for His own glory.

Again, in various different passages, Jesus is careful to emphasize that the Holy Spirit is a real Person—just as really so as God the Father and God the Son. For example, in John chapter 16, verse 13, Jesus says: "How-beit when he, the Spirit of truth, is come, he will guide you into all truth: for he shall not speak of himself; but what-soever he shall hear, that shall he speak . . ." Here Jesus emphasizes the personality of the Holy Spirit in two ways: first, by using the pronoun "he" (rather than "it"); second, by attributing to the Holy Spirit the ability to speak. Re-flection will show that the ability to speak is one of the decisive, distinguishing features of personality. To any-thing capable of speaking for itself we naturally attribute the concept of a person; but if anything lacks this ability to speak, we should not normally consider it a person. The fact that the Holy Spirit speaks directly for Himself is one of the great marks of His true personality.

Side by side with this we must set the words of Paul in First Corinthians, chapter 6, verse 19: "What? know ye not that your body is the temple of the Holy Ghost which is in you . . .?" Here Paul teaches that the physical body of the redeemed believer is the appointed temple in which the Holy Spirit desires to dwell. Appropriately therefore, the evidence that the Holy Spirit, as a Person, has come to take up His dwelling in this physical temple is that He exercises the attribute of personality and speaks from within the temple, using the tongue and the lips of the believer himself to make this speech audible.

So it was also in the tabernacle of Moses. In Numbers chapter 7, verse 89, we read that when Moses went into the tabernacle to commune with God, "then he heard the voice of one speaking unto him from the mercy seat." Because Moses heard this voice—the mark of personality—he knew that the Person of the Lord Himself was present in the tabernacle. In like manner today, when we hear the voice of the Holy Spirit speaking audibly from within the temple of a believer's body, we know, by this evidence of personality, that the Holy Spirit Himself—the Third Person of the Godhead—has taken up residence within the believer.

We find, then, that speaking with other tongues as the evidence of the baptism in the Holy Spirit, accords with three great principles of scripture.

First, the heart of the believer, supernaturally filled with the Holy Spirit, overflows supernaturally through his mouth.

Second, the evidence that the believer has yielded his physical members to God, is that God's Spirit controls that member—the tongue—which the believer cannot control for himself.

Third, by speaking from within the temple of the believer's body, the Holy Spirit demonstrates that He now dwells there as a Person.

* * *

In our next book* we shall go on to examine some of the main purposes for which the baptism in the Holy Spirit is given.

* Published under the title: "Purposes Of Pentecost".
See back cover of this book.

MESSAGES AVAILABLE ON CASSETTE
$4.95 each

SPIRITUAL CONFLICT ALBUM I	1001	How Conflict Began: The Pre-Adamic Period
	1002	The Rebellion of Lucifer
	1003	Results Produced by Lucifer's Rebellion
	1004	The Adamic Race: Five Unique Features
	1005	Adam's Fall and its Results
	1006	Results of Adam's Fall (cont'd)
SPIRITUAL CONFLICT ALBUM II	1007	Jesus The Last Adam
	1008	The Exchange Made at the Cross
	1009	Jesus Tasted Death in all its Phases
	1010	The Cross Cancelled Satan's Claims
	1011	Jesus the Second Man
	1012	God's Purpose for the New Race
SPIRITUAL CONFLICT ALBUM III	1013	Five Ways Christ Undoes Satan's Work
	1014	God's Program for the Close of the Age—Part I
	1015	God's Program for the Close of the Age—Part II
	1016	Satan's Program for the Close of the Age
	1017	Restraining And Casting Down Satan
	1018	Spiritual Weapons: The Blood, The Word, Our Testimony
EFFECTIVE PRAYING	4001	Seven Basic Conditions for Answered Prayer
	4002	Intervening By Prayer in National Affairs
	4003	Fasting Precipitates God's Latter Rain
	4004	Spiritual Weapons For Spiritual Warfare
	4005	God's Atomic Weapon: The Blood of Jesus
	4006	Epilogue: The Glorious Church
PROPHECY	7001	Climax in four phases: Repentance, Refreshing, Restoration, Return of Christ
	7002	Divine Destiny for this Nation (USA) and this generation
	7003	Prophecy: God's Time Map
	7004	Israel and the Church: Parallel Restoration

- **Each Message is approximately one hour in length.**
- **A printed verse-by-verse analysis and outline is included with every tape.**

OVER 115 MESSAGES ARE AVAILABLE—WRITE FOR FREE CATALOG